Improvement and Accountability

also in the Higher Education Policy Series

Self-Regulation in Higher Education
A Multi-National Perspective on Collaborative Systems of Quality
  Assurance and Control
H.R. Kells
ISBN 1 85302 528 3
Higher Education Policy Series 15

Assessing Quality in Further and Higher Education
Allan Ashworth and Roger Harvey
ISBN 1 85302 539 9
Higher Education Policy Series 24

The Use of Performance Indicators in Higher Education
A Critical Analysis of Developing Practice
2nd edition
Martin Cave, Stephen Hanney and Maurice Kogan
ISBN 1 85302 518 6
Higher Education Policy Series 3

Evaluating Higher Education
Edited by Maurice Kogan
ISBN 1 85302 510 0
Higher Education Policy Series 6

Dimensions of Evaluation in Higher Education
Report of the IMHE Study Group on Evaluation in Higher Education
Urban Dahllöf, John Harris, Michael Shattock, André Staropoli and
Roeland in't Veld
ISBN 1 85302 526 7
Higher Education Policy Series 13

Higher Education Policy Series 30

Improvement and Accountability: Navigating between Scylla and Charybdis

Guide for External Quality Assessment in Higher Education

A.I. Vroeijenstijn

Jessica Kingsley Publishers
London and Bristol, Pennsylvania

The views expressed in this book stress the dual function of External Quality Assessment: quality improvement and accountability. Managing the EQA process is like navigating between two extremes: aiming only at improvement, the system will be shipwrecked against Scylla because the outside stakeholders will ask for accountability and design their own EQA system; placing too much emphasis on accountability, the system will come up against Charybdis, because improvement will be hindered or even made impossible. It will be necessary to look for an effective relationship between improvement orientation and accountability. This will be a difficult, but not impossible, task.

The views expressed by the author are his own. They do not necessarily represent those of his employer, the Association of Universities in the Netherlands (VSNU) or its individual members.

First published in the United Kingdom in 1995 by
Jessica Kingsley Publishers Ltd
116 Pentonville Road
London N1 9JB, England
and
1900 Frost Road, Suite 101
Bristol, PA 19007, U S A

Copyright © 1995 A.I. Vroeijenstijn

Library of Congress Cataloging in Publication Data
A CIP catalogue record for this book is available from the Library of Congress

British Library Cataloguing in Publication Data
A CIP catalogue record for this book is available from the British Library

ISBN 1-85302-546-1

Printed and Bound in Great Britain by
Cromwell Press, Melksham, Wiltshire

Contents

List of Tables

List of Figures

For Henriëtte

Preface

Sometimes people may think there is talk of a new disease at the moment: the Quality disease. It seems that the Q-virus has affected and contaminated the whole world, from North to South, from West to East. Or is it a new religion: Quality written with a capital and with a whole new caste of high priests, serving Quality Assessment? Is it in vogue to talk Quality language?

Through the heavy emphasis on quality during the last years, people could think that quality is only an invention of the last decade, as if higher education institutions had no interest in quality before politicians put it on the agenda. On the contrary, higher education has always paid attention to quality. To deliver quality is innate in the academic attitude. So far there is nothing new under the sun. Except that formerly, quality assessment was often still labelled as 'evaluation', trying to discover bottlenecks and weak spots and trying to find good solutions for them. The attention to quality was intrinsic and inward-oriented. The outside world was unwittingly left out.

However in the 1980s, quality assessment got a public function too. The outside world exerted pressure on the higher education institutions to become accountable for quality and for money spent. Many governments have abandoned the idea of a strongly centrally regulated system of higher education, as had been normal in most European countries, and are willing to give more autonomy to the institutions provided that quality will be guaranteed.

Therefore, all over the world we see a growing focus of attention on quality assessment. Higher education institutions are starting, whether or not forced by the actions of government, to think about systems for external quality assessment (EQA), with which the old intrinsic function may be strengthened and the rising public function may be shaped.

In looking for a system of EQA, people may have special aims in mind: it might serve as an accreditation system for institutions or programmes; it might serve a performance-based funding system; or it might help in deciding on allocation of money or accounting for money spent.

Without being detrimental to other approaches, in this book a system of EQA has been chosen which:

- is owned by higher education institutions themselves, although sanctioned by the government

- aims foremost at quality assurance, quality enhancement and quality improvement, while trying also to shape the public function

- is in the first instance programme-oriented. However, institutional audit is a natural keystone of the system.

This choice has been made purposely, because quality assessment will always be a time-consuming and expensive activity, which may give higher education a lot of advantages, but will also cause problems. Therefore we have to look for a system of EQA that has the greatest chance of success and real benefits. Quality only can be assured by those who are responsible for the quality: the staff and students of the higher education institutions. This means that the higher education institutions should believe in the system and not that it should be conceived as a threat. The system should also orient itself towards those areas in which it will have the most direct effect: the teaching and learning environment (the programme or curriculum) and the research programmes. EQA should primarily be an instrument for quality assurance and quality improvement and not for control. It serves foremost the higher education institutions and not the inspectorate or government.

However, EQA also has a public function: accountability and information for the outside world. It will not always be easy to combine improvement and accountability. Being responsible for the system of EQA is like navigating between Scylla and Charybdis. Is it possible to reconcile the irreconcilable? Aiming only at improvement, the system will be shipwrecked against the Scylla because the outside stakeholders will ask for accountability and design their own EQA-system. Overemphasizing accountability, the system will disappear in the Charybdis, because improvement will be hindered or even made impossible. It is necessary to look for an effective relation between improvement and accountability. This will be a hard, but not impossible, task.

This book is directed at managers of higher education institutions, deans of faculties and heads of divisions, administrators and policy makers, and also interested staff members and students: in short, everyone who is confronted with the question of external quality assessment. The purpose of this book is to hold out a hand for everyone who is thinking about the design of a system for external quality assessment. Even if one chooses an approach to EQA which is different from the above-mentioned 'improvement orientation', it can be worthwhile to use the ideas expressed in this book. Although the 'why' may differ, the 'how' will be more or less the same.

The book is not an academic, theoretical essay about quality and quality assessment, but a pragmatic guide with advice and recommendations based on five years' extensive experience in Dutch universities. Although the Dutch 'model' (if we may speak about a model) attracts much attention, it will be clear that it is not possible to copy the working method without changes. The system should be adapted to the objectives in mind and to the national context, just as the Association of Universities in the Netherlands (VSNU) 'shopped around' the world in 1985/1986 and then designed a system of EQA tailored for the Dutch universities.

This handbook is particularly about the assessment of the quality of teaching/learning. Assessment of research will only be mentioned occasionally. There are several reasons for this. One of them is that there are already well established systems of research assessment. In research there is a long tradition of a scholarly community, in which scholars criticize each other at conferences, seminars, etc. There also exists a long tradition of peer review, assessing articles for scientific journals. Furthermore, researchers and their proposals are being assessed by funding councils when they apply for grants. None of these assessments apply to the field of teaching and learning. On the other hand, we do see development of a more integral quality assessment for research.

Chapter 1 deals with several general questions which must be answered before the design of an EQA system can begin. It also contains a number of basic principles of a good, functioning system. Chapter 2 gives an outline of a system of external quality assessment. In Chapter 3 clear guidelines are given for self-assessment, while Chapter 4 contains guidelines for the review committee. While Chapters 1 and 2 are for reading, Chapters 3 and 4 form a real manual for an agency in charge of the execution of EQA, for the unit to be assessed and for the review committee which is going to assess it. In combination with the appendices it contains the tools for a good functioning system of EQA. Chapter 5 places quality assessment in a European framework and discusses the European dimension in EQA.

How to use this book:

- Do not copy the system blindly, but adapt it to your own purposes needs and circumstances. In a given context some aspects will be more important than others.

- The described method and the sketched procedures result from a process of trial and error over five years and are the outcomes of an iterative process. Starting with little or no experience in EQA it may not be possible to apply all the rules of the game, because one has first to learn to cope with the whole idea of EQA. It is like skiing: after the first lessons one is not yet able to practise the techniques needed for a black run. However, you have to apply at least the basic principles if you ever want to take the black run. So it is with EQA: start just with the basics, but keep in mind the direction you want to go in. Keep also in mind that autonomy and quality assurance are two sides of the same coin. Therefore the higher education institutions are responsible for internal and external quality assessment; do not leave it to outsiders.

Quite in the spirit of the subject of this book, I have asked an external panel to assess the quality of the manuscript. I am indebted to my colleagues at VSNU, in one way or another involved in quality assessment: Marianne van der Weiden, Ad Verkley, Jacques Houben and Frank van Eijkern. I have also asked some people from the target group: Dirk Jan Melker (The Haagse Hoge School), Alberto Amaral (Rector of the University of Oporto), António Simões Lopes (Rector of the Technical University of Lisbon), Peter Brandon (Pro-Vice-Chancellor of the University of Salford), Roland Richter (Wissenschaftliches Sekretariat für Studienreform im Land Nordrhein-Westfalen), Sami Kanaan (Gesellschaft für Hochschule und Forschung) and Airi Rovio-Johanson (Göteborg University). They have all made very valuable comments and recommendations. My thanks especially go to my wife Henriëtte, who stimulated me to write the book and made very valuable comments on the first draft. Without her I should never have been able to devote so much time to the fascinating subject of quality assessment. Therefore this book is dedicated to her.

A. I. Vroeijenstijn
February 1994

Some Terms Explained

In transferring experiences from elsewhere, it is not enough to translate a text. Understanding is not only a matter of language, but also involves understanding the cultural context. One needs to adapt terms to one's own setting. Therefore some terms used in this book which may have a different meaning in another context are explained here. To make it easier to place the terminology in the reader's environment, in Appendix 1 a short description of the Dutch university system is given.

Quality assurance

Quality assurance may be described as systematic, structured and continuous attention to quality in terms of quality maintenance and quality improvement. Continuous quality care is a *sine qua non* for quality assurance. One of the tools in the field of quality care is quality assessment.

Quality assessment

By quality assessment we mean every structured activity which leads to a judgement of the quality of the teaching/learning process and/or research, whether self-assessment or assessment by external experts. There is no real difference between assessment, evaluation and review. Those terms are seen as interchangeable.

Quality audit

Quality audit has a more strict meaning and aim at the process of evaluating the way quality is assured. It is not so much looking for quality, more to a quality assurance mechanism.

Review committee

One of the pillars of external quality assessment is peer review: a group of experts from outside the higher education institution will assess the faculty. In this book this group is called the review committee. In the literature we also find the terms assessment committee, visiting committee and expert committee are all used to express the same meaning.

Faculty

The faculty is the unit in the higher education institution responsible for a programme (see below). We talk about the Faculty of Economics, Faculty of Medicine, etc. It is interchangeable with Department or School.

Programme, curriculum, course

By programme we mean a coherent set of courses, leading to a certain degree. In a programme we can distinguish a core curriculum and optional courses, together making up the different ways a student can choose to arrive at the degree. By programme review we mean assessing all teaching and learning activities leading to a particular degree.

Discipline

When talking about discipline review, we mean the review in a special subject field like Psychology, Economics, Law. The assessment of the discipline Law will include several programmes or curricula, e.g. private law, public law, international law.

Examinations and student assessment

When talking about exams and examinations people often have final examinations in mind. But there are also yearly examinations or preliminary examinations, to be taken at the end of a course, a semester or trimester. In this book we mean the assessment of the students in one way or another as part of and counting for the final degree exam.

Chapter 1

New Interest in Quality Assessment in Higher Education

Nowadays there is a lot of discussion about quality. In many countries higher education is involved in a quality debate. Governments are pressing the higher education institutions to pay more attention to, and to be accountable for, quality.

Often the message is: more autonomy and freedom for the higher education institutions if quality is assured by a good, functioning system of external quality assessment (EQA), which not only contributes to quality maintenance and quality enhancement, but also provides public insight into quality. So, in many countries, governments and higher education institutions are thinking about the design of an EQA system.

Before a system for quality assessment can be designed, it is necessary to face some questions to prevent needless discussions and unwanted debates. Decisions have to be made to prevent obscurity or disagreement. In this chapter the following questions will be treated:

- Why is so much attention being paid to quality?
- What may be expected from external quality assessment?
- What is quality?
- What is the relationship between level, standards and quality?
- Can quality be measured? What is the role of performance indicators?
- How can one choose between institutional review, departmental review or programme review?

- Should assessment of teaching and assessment of research be in tandem or not?
- Should there be a connection with funding?
- Which is appropriate: horizontal and comparative or an individual assessment?
- Government and higher education institutions: opponents or allies?

At the end of the chapter some basic principles for an effective system of external quality assessment will be given.

1.1 Why is so Much Attention Being Paid to Quality?

Nowadays quality is in the limelight all over the world. Everybody in all sectors of society is talking about it: industry, service centres, hospitals; and, of course, education cannot escape. There is much public discussion on the quality of education (or perhaps discussion on the assumed lack of quality), including higher education.

There is so much attention being paid to quality that people may think that it is an invention of the last decade and that there was no notion of quality before 1985. But of course this is not true. The concept of quality is not new: it has always been part of academic tradition. It is the outside world that now emphasizes the need for explicit attention to quality. Several reasons can be given:

- Since the 1950s, there has been talk of mass higher education. More and more students are enrolling in higher education, causing pressure on the national budgets. Expenditure per student is much lower. The government must assure society that this does not endanger quality. This problem has been aggravated by economic recessions. On behalf of society, governments have wanted a better insight into costs and benefits of higher education. Higher education, in their view, cost too much or was not efficient enough (Moodie 1986, Barnett 1992).

- The relationship between higher education and society has changed in the last decades. Society has become more and more interested in higher education. The relationship between higher education and the labour market has become a topic for discussion. In some disciplines, e.g. in social sciences, psychology and history, there are a lot of students, but few available jobs. The unemployment figures are high. In other disciplines like engineering there is often a shortage of students and society could use more graduates. Such a situation causes pressure on higher education to steer the student flow in the wanted direction.

- Quality has become more and more important for the higher education institutions, because the question is whether it is still possible to deliver the same quality within the given boundary conditions. Since the 1950s one can talk of a 'quality gap': on the one hand, governments are striving to increase the numbers of students enrolled (higher education for as many as possible); on the other hand we see a continuous decrease in investments. Higher education institutions have to do more with less money. But at the same time quality is expected to be maintained or to improve (Barnett 1992).

- Student exchanges and international cooperation require insight into quality. There always has been a exchange of students between countries. However, since the introduction of programmes like ERASMUS, it has become increasingly clear that it is very important to know about the quality in the other faculty. Questions have to be asked, such as: 'Can I recognize the course?' or 'Is it good enough?' Also the European Union with a open labour market asks for insight into the quality of the curricula and the standards of the graduates.

- Governments have always assigned themselves a strong steering role in the development of higher education. The dominant thought was that it should be possible to develop higher education by detailed regulations. Since the 1980s governments have abandoned the idea of the 'makable society' and a new philosophy with regard to higher education policy has arisen. This new philosophy is also caused because with mass access to higher education the system has become so complex that central control has appeared as inefficient. Also the very rapid

change of scientific and technological knowledge
necessitated a more flexible system, so that many
decisions could be made at local (institutional) level.
Therefore in many European countries governments are
stepping back and promising more autonomy to higher
education. However, in exchange, the governments
require quality assurance.

In short, society requires accountability and quality assurance and
is asking for value for money. Governments are willing to grant
more institutional autonomy, provided quality is assured. Therefore we see in many countries a discussion on quality, quality
maintenance, quality assurance and quality assessment.

1.2 Autonomy and Quality Assurance: Two Sides of the Same Coin

One of the reasons for the increasing attention to quality and
quality assessment in the outside world is the change in the
attitude of governments regarding higher education policy, as
pointed out in Section 1.1. Such a development can be seen in many
European countries. We will sketch the developments in the Netherlands as an example, but the reader will recognize the ideas of
his or her own government.

In the Netherlands it started in 1985. A new era began with
regard to the higher education policy of the Dutch government.
The Ministry of Higher Education and Science published the
policy document *Higher Education: Autonomy and Quality* (HOAK)
(Ministerie van Onderwijs en Wetenschappen 1985). Much has
already been published about the content and the consequences of
this document (see, for example, van Vught 1988, 1989).

The following analysis has been given:

In the HOAK policy document the minister presented a
new governmental strategy towards higher education.
The new attitude indicates an important break with the
traditional governmental strategy, which was a strategy
of detailed planning and control. In the years before 1985
government tried to steer the higher education system
with stringent regulations and extensive control-mecha-
nisms. Government saw itself as an omnipotent actor
who thought to be able to guide the higher education

system according to its own objectives. The new strategy appears to be an important change. By strengthening the autonomy of the higher education institutions, government claims to create fruitful conditions for the enlargement of the adaptive power and flexibility of higher education institutions to respond to the needs of society.

By strengthening the institutional autonomy government also claims to stimulate the levels of quality and differentiation of the higher education system. The new governmental strategy was based on the idea that the increase of the institutional autonomy will result in an improvement of the quality of the higher education system. (Maassen and van Vught 1989 pp.113–128)

But with regard to the autonomy of the higher education institutions the question arises whether this autonomy is real, or a fake or restricted autonomy. Autonomy and self-regulation for higher education institutions have been promised, but at the same time the government has set bounds to them: 'Certain forms of behaviour by the institutions cannot be allowed' (Maassen and van Vught 1989). The government has its own goals for higher education and still wishes to steer its development. Instead of giving the responsibilities to the higher education institutions and them stepping back, the government has an attitude of 'remote control'. Instead of being autonomous, the Dutch universities are in imminent danger of becoming puppets.

According to the HOAK document, quality was the responsibility of the higher education institutions and they were therefore accountable for their internal evaluation. They should report on their evaluation in annual documents. However, the government felt the need for an independent assessment of the performance of the higher education institutes. This should be done by independent experts and an independent authority. The government decided upon a system of review committees to be organised by an Inspectorate for Higher Education (Ministerie van Onderwijs en Wetenschappen 1985), and subsequently an Inspectorate for the Universities was installed in 1985 next to the already existing Inspectorate for Higher Vocational Education (HBO).[1]

---

1   In 1985 Higher Vocational Education was regulated by the Secondary Education Act, and was therefore already subject to an Inspectorate.

The task of the Inspectorate was:

1. to organise and support external quality assessment
2. to be informed about the state of the art of the higher education system, among other things, by visiting the institutions
3. to oversee the observation of rules and regulations
4. to advise the Minister and formulate proposals
5. to contribute to the development of higher education.

Summarizing, we can say that the *internal quality assessment* was declared the responsibility of the higher education institutions and the *external quality assessment* was declared that of the Inspectorate. However, the reality has turned out differently. The universities, under the umbrella of the recently founded Association of Universities in the Netherlands (VSNU), did not keep quiet. Greater autonomy and more freedom for their own programmes were welcomed. Autonomy and quality assurance as two sides of the same coin were not disputed by anybody. But the higher education institutions could not agree to external quality assessment being a task of an authority outside the institutions themselves. In the opinion of the universities, quality and quality assurance, including the external part, is first and foremost the responsibility of the institutions themselves. The higher education institutions should be the 'owners' of the system, not the Minister or the Inspectorate.

In a meeting between the Minister of Higher Education and Sciences and the higher education institutions in April 1986 it was agreed that the institutions would take care of quality assessment through evaluation. They would do that by internal evaluation and by periodical external quality assessment. The institutions would develop a coordinated and public external quality assessment system, focusing on the main tasks of the institutions: education, research and public services.

The agreements were fixed in the Higher Education and Research Act. Article 1.18 reads:

1. The administration of an institution...shall ensure that arrangements are made, as far as possible in collaboration with other institutions, for regular assessment, partly by independent experts, of the quality of the institution's work. The assessment of higher education institutions shall include the opinion of students on the quality of

teaching in the institution. In so far as the assessment is carried out by independent experts, the results of the assessment shall be made public.

2. Our Minister shall supervise the implementation of the provisions of subsection 1. He may ask for a study to be made of the quality of the institution's work... (Ministry of Education and Science 1993)

Looking at the Act, we may conclude that the formulation is in agreement with the idea of remote control by the government. Detailed regulations for a system of external quality assessment are lacking. The Act only stipulates that:

- there has to be a system of quality assessment
- external experts have to be involved
- the opinion of students has to be involved
- the outcomes of external assessment are made public.

We see in some countries a tendency for governments to regulate EQA in a very detailed way and fix processes and procedures by law. Such an approach is best avoided. Of course some regulation by law is important, but too many detailed regulations make the system of EQA inflexible towards necessary adaptations. If higher education institutions take care to develop a good functioning system of EQA, there will be no need for detailed regulation by law.

1.3 Why External Quality Assessment?

There are different motives for deciding upon external quality assessment (EQA). In some cases a threshold quality may be required before a programme or an institute can be accredited. In other cases the comparative quality of different programmes (for ranking) is sought, for example because the government wants to know where to allocate the money or when reallocation is necessary. EQA can also be used to discover weak and strong spots and, in so doing, improve the education offered.

Government is interested in EQA because it has a constitutional obligation to assure the quality of education and because it is called to account to parliament for the money spent on higher education. Government also wants to find out how far its own aims are being realized, for example in achieving mass higher education, or regarding the role of universities in technological developments, or in increasing the participation rate for women.

Government is interested in demonstrating to society at large, and parliament in particular, that it is in control of higher education and makes justifiable decisions with regard to allocation of money, termination of programmes, etc. So the government's problem is how to 'prove' that the right decisions are being made wherever changes in the boundary conditions might affect quality. If those effects could be measured and compared, such 'proof' may become feasible. Performance indicators are thus regarded as very helpful in assessing the outcome of governmental and institutional policies (Vroeijenstijn and Acherman 1990).

For the government EQA means collecting as much objective information as possible with regard to the performance of the higher education institutions and as much objective measurement of the quality. Therefore, ministers are often eager to have a definition of a set of performance indicators. A malevolent person could summarize the ideas of many ministers about quality assessment in the following way: 'Define what quality is, set standards for it, take some performance indicators and measure to what extent the standards are reached. On that basis you can make decisions'. Such a view of EQA presupposes three things, namely: that quality can be defined; that performance indicators have a relation with quality; and that quality can be quantified and objectified. We will return to this later on.

Looking at governmental policy papers, we find they use the terms 'quality control' and 'quality measurement'. Control and measurement are summative in nature and convey the idea of punishment or reward. 'Quality control is inherently punitive, imposing sanctions for inadequacy, but at the same time it implies that once a minimum acceptable level has been reached no further effort for improvement is needed' (Lynton 1988).

The concerns of the higher education institutions are whether it is possible to offer high quality education within the conditions set by the government and how to convince the public that the faculties are providing the best quality possible (under the circumstances). The goal is quality improvement where possible and the main question how to ensure that teaching is adapted to changing boundary conditions. To quote Henry Mintzberg (1983): 'Change in the professional bureaucracy (like universities) does not sweep in from new administrators taking office to announce major reforms, nor from government technostructures intent on bringing the professionals under their control. Rather, change seeps in by the slow process of changing the professionals...' So the question is how to change the attitude of professionals with regard to their contributions to a particular educational programme. In other words, to whom will they listen? The obvious answer is that they are willing to listen to their peers, and the basic answer to programme improvement is peer review, rather than 'control' by administrators, inspectors or the like.

However, quality improvement is not an end in itself. Quality improvement serves another more distant goal. The ultimate aim is delivering quality and by doing so forming good graduates, attracting more students and more finance and also gaining more prestige.

Table 1.1 summarizes the different views on EQA. Opposite the summative approach of EQA from the government side stands the more formative approach of the universities. Here, the starting point is that EQA especially aims at quality improvement. The most important function is an analysis of strengths and weaknesses and actions for improvement, based on this analysis.

The universities also emphasize the accountability function of EQA and believe that the outcome of EQA should play a role in the process of self-regulation, internal steering and quality assurance.

All expectations regarding external quality assessment are legitimate and the characteristics of an EQA system must be adapted to its objectives. For instance, it is not possible to provide accountability without external review or quality improvement without self-evaluation. But do we need an elaborate system of EQA for all the objectives (accreditation, accountability, resource allocation, steering, etc.)? We should be very careful about burdening the higher education institutions with continual assessments. Sometimes faculties are overwhelmed by all the attention nowadays on quality. There is no time left to work on quality because the faculty has to continually provide evidence of it. The question is whether there is always a need for a separate system of EQA for each objective, or whether some of the systems can be combined.

Table 1.1. Views on External Quality Assessment

	Government	HE Institutions
Nature of EQA	*Summative*	*Formative*
Aims	accreditation (threshold quality)	quality improvement
	accountability to parliament (value for money)	accountability
	steering/planning of HE: are the aims of the government with regard to HE reached?	self-regulation
		quality assurance
	constitutional 'assurance of quality'	
	comparison/ranking in the light of funding	
	efficiency	
	information for students and employers	
Instruments	inspectorate	self-assessment
	performance Indicators	peer review

Accreditation

When accreditation is wanted for a institution as a whole or for a specific programme, we can make use of the system of EQA outlined in this book. It will also be based on self-assessment and peer review. The only difference will be that the frame of reference of the committee (see Section 4.2), the criteria and standards against which the institution or programme will be assessed, are formulated by an outside body, whether the government on behalf of the tax-payer, or a professional body on behalf of the profession. There is no need for an accreditation system as well an improvement-oriented EQA system.

Funding

We also do not need an EQA system for funding. Most funding systems will be based on a mixture of input and output financing: number of students entering the programme combined with number of graduates. For such a funding system we do not need to assess the quality beforehand. However, quality of output will be questioned. Certain guarantees for the quality may be built in by coupling a certain percentage of the budget with the request to participate in one way or another in EQA.

Accountability

Society demands value for money. Therefore the institutions are accountable for the money spent, which is a normal request. However, rendering an account of money spent should be done in the annual reports of the institutions. Government and institutions should agree upon the data the institute has to publish, e.g. enrolment figures, drop-outs, number of graduates, cost per student, research efforts. However, the EQA system should not be burdened with those questions. Of course EQA will provide the information to be used in the framework of accountability, but the external assessment plays only a partial role in accountability and pays particular attention to the way an institution or a faculty copes with quality and quality assurance.

Achievement of governmental goals and planning

Government likes to know whether its goals are being realized or not. It likes also to have information for the planning and steering of the higher education system. This, however, should not be the main purpose of EQA. Government can require the institutions to give the information needed in the annual reports. The public reports of the EQA might be one of the resources by which the wanted information is obtained, without directly linking the assessment with this purpose.

Information for students and employers

Here, the same may be said as with governmental policy: the way of publishing the reports of EQA might be useful, but should not be made a main aim.

Quality improvement

For quality improvement there is a need for critical self-assessment and an open discussion with peers. There should not be a direct threat from outside, hindering the discussion. The system described in this book is mostly aimed at quality improvement, but may also address accountability, provided one is agreed about the relationship between improvement and accountability.

Looking at the literature and the experiences in different countries, one thing is for sure: it must be clear to every party concerned what is to be expected from EQA. The system of EQA should not be burdened too much. Summative and formative assessment require a different approach. Most of the information the government wants can be obtained in other ways or by *ad hoc* assessment. The involvement of summative aspects in EQA may be a threat to the formative approach: it is difficult for EQA to serve two masters (Vroeijenstijn 1992).

1.4 What is Quality?

It is a waste of time to look for a definition

Everybody thinking about quality assessment is faced with the question, 'What is quality?' Many discussions on quality start with a quotation from the book *Zen and the Art of Motorcycle Maintenance*:

> Quality...you know what it is, yet you don't know what it is. But that's self-contradictory. But some things are better than others, that is, they have more quality. But when you try to say what the quality is, apart from the things that have it, it all goes poof! There's nothing to talk about. But if you can't say what Quality is, how do we know what it is, or how do you know that it even exists? If no one knows what it is, then for all practical purposes it doesn't exist at all. But for practical purposes it really does exist. What else are the grades based on? Why else would people pay fortunes for some things and throw others in the trash pile? Obviously some things are better than others...but what's the 'betterness'? So round and round you go, spinning mental wheels and nowhere finding any place to get traction. What the hell is Quality? What is it? (Pirsig 1974)

In spite of those reflections of Pirsig's, many books and articles are written, trying to discover the nature of quality. But quality is like love. Everybody talks about it and everybody knows what he or she is talking about. Everybody knows and feels when there is love. Everybody recognizes it. But when we try to give a definition of it, we are left standing with empty hands.

In the literature we find several descriptions of the concept of quality. Sometimes quality is defined as 'fitness for purpose' (Ball 1985). Quality is also defined in terms of added value (McClain *et al.* 1989, Ashworth and Harvey 1994). Another often-used description is: 'Something has quality when it meets the expectations of the consumer/user; quality is the satisfaction of the client'. Harvey and Green (1993) try to describe the nature of the concept of quality in relation to higher education. After a thorough treatise, they conclude: 'First, quality means different things to different people. Second, quality is relative to "processes" or "outcomes".'

If talking about a concrete product we want to buy, for example a computer, it is easy to define quality: it has to do with what we expect it will do. There will be no misunderstanding. But when we consider education, we have trouble. Who is the client? Who is the consumer? When the government considers quality, it looks first to the pass/fail ratio, the dropouts and enrolment time. Quality in governments' eyes can be described as, 'As many students as possible finishing the programme in the scheduled time with a degree of an international standard with reduced costs.'

Employers, talking about quality, will refer to the knowledge, skills and attitudes obtained during the period of study: the 'product' that is tested is the graduate.

Quality of education has a totally different meaning in the eyes of the students. For them, quality is connected with the contribution to individual development and the preparation for a position in society. Education must link up with the personal interest of the student. But the educational process also has to be organized in such a way that he or she can finish the study in the given time.

The academic will define quality as, 'A good academic training based on good knowledge transfer and a good learning environment and a good relationship between teaching and research.'

The view on quality is also fixed by people's concept of higher education. Do people see higher education as the production of qualified manpower or as training for a research career? Is higher education conceived as the efficient management of teaching provision or is higher education a matter of extending life chances (Barnett 1993)?

We must conclude that quality is a very complex concept (see Table 1.2). We cannot speak of 'the quality'; we have to speak about 'qualities'.

Table 1.2. Aspects of Quality and Stakeholders

Stakeholder	Students	Employers	Government	HE institution	Staff
Aspect of quality					
Input (for example):					
student intake			*	*	*
selection	*		*	*	*
budget				*	*
academic staff	*			*	
Process (for example):					
aims/goals	*		(*)	*	*
educational process	*			*	*
educational organisation	*			*	*
content	*		*	*	
counselling	*			*	
Output (for example):					
pass/fail rate	*		*	*	
the graduate	*	*	*	*	*

We must make a distinction between quality requirements set by the student, the academic world, by the labour market/society and by the government. But there are not only different qualities; we must also consider different aspects of quality. So there is quality of input, process quality and quality of output. Quality assessment has to take into account all these dimensions. Therefore it is a waste of time to try to define quality precisely. There does not exist an absolute quality.

Quality is a matter of negotiating between all parties concerned. Every stakeholder should formulate, as clearly as possible, its requirements. The higher education institution or faculty, as ultimate supplier, must try to reconcile all those different wishes and requirements. Sometimes the expectations will run parallel, but they can conflict just as well. As far as possible, the requirements of all stakeholders should be translated in the mission, the goals and the objectives of a faculty and of the educational programme (and as far as it concerns research, in the research programmes).

If this is done, then we say that a faculty or university has 'quality' (see Figure 1.1). Although it remains necessary to strive at a good description of the different requirements and aspects of quality, the lack of a definition should never be an excuse not to pay attention to quality or to work for quality enhancement.

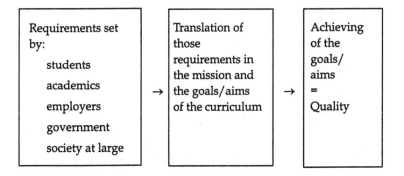

Figure 1.1. Quality as a matter of negotiating between parties concerned

If we have to describe quality we may say that 'quality will be specified by the outcomes of the negotiations between all parties concerned about the expected requirements. Higher Education should try to fulfil as much as possible all wishes and this will have to be shown in the formulation of the goals and aims.'

In the discussions on the nature of quality, we see a lot of misconceptions and a blending of concepts.

Quality is not always the same as efficiency!

The discussion on quality assessment is often connected with the concept 'efficiency' (saving money, making a more rational use of public resources). In assessing quality, an important question will be, 'Do we achieve the required level of quality with acceptable costs?' An efficiency-oriented approach as such is a good starting point, but the problem is that efficiency is not always defined as 'against acceptable costs' but often as 'against minimal costs' and this may be a threat to quality. It may be very efficient to have lectures for a thousand students, but it is not effective. It may be considered efficient to have a very structured study programme with student assessments every four weeks, forcing students to work and to keep up with the programme. However, do we create with this method the 'right', independent, critically thinking graduate? It may be considered as efficient to use multiple choice questions for student assessment, but does it enhance verbal and written communication skills?

Quality is not the same as being excellent!

Often quality is mixed up with being excellent. Even Pirsig makes a mistake by saying 'some things are better than others, that is, they have more quality.' Frequently people talking about promoting *quality*, mean promoting *excellence*. However, quality is not the same as being excellent. Of course, everybody likes to do his/her best to deliver quality, but not every institution can be a Yale or a MIT. A country with only excellent universities does not exist; there can only be some excellent universities if there is a high number of average universities. An institution can make the choice not to aim at being 'excellent', because it likes to educate many students and not only the brightest ones. A typical regional university will probably make a different choice from an institute like Berkeley. We can talk about good, better and best, or good, better and excellent. But we should not talk about good quality, better quality and excellent quality.

Level, standards and quality

In striving for quality we will say: 'We will do what we promise to do.' McDonald's, for example, will strive for quality, and when we take a fast food dinner we will probably get quality. However, this is not the same level of quality as we will get when we have dinner in a restaurant with one or two stars in the *Guide de Michelin*. So we cannot assess the quality of McDonald's against the same criteria as those with which we assess a star restaurant. Every level of quality has its price. The only common feature is that we may ask, 'Will we get what we expect?'

Within the framework of EQA, clear distinctions also have to be made between level, standards and quality. Too often these three concepts are confused:

LEVEL

A programme leading to a Master's degree is of a higher level than a programme leading to a Bachelor's degree. But this does not mean that the quality of the Master's programme is higher.

STANDARDS

For each programme it is possible to define standards, or minimum requirements to be expected from the graduates. Standards can be described as a statement in general or specific terms of the knowledge, understanding, skills and attitude to be demonstrated by successful graduates. The question is whether or not a programme with high standards and a low number of graduates has high quality.

QUALITY

Quality is much broader and includes standards as well as the processes of teaching and learning, the activities of departments and institutions and the congruence between the goals of a programme and the competence of its graduates (Frazer 1992, 1994).

1.5 Can Quality be Measured? What is the Role of Performance Indicators?

Criteria and standards are also subject to negotiation

Other topics in the discussion on external quality assessment are criteria and standards. If one looks at what is said about quality, it will be obvious that it is impossible to identify one set of criteria or standards for quality of higher education. The parties concerned will have their own criteria and norms derived from their own objectives and/or demands. This means that government will formulate other criteria than, for example, employers.

In the framework of EQA it is impossible to formulate beforehand overall criteria for higher education. They will differ from discipline to discipline. The expectations of the labour market will play a totally different role in assessing philosophy or assessing electrical engineering. The criteria of the different partners may actually be in conflict. Government may put forward as one of the criteria: 'the programme must be organised in such a way that students can finish the programme with a minimum of dropout and within the given time'; or 'the success ratio of the first year should be 70 per cent'. But these criteria may clash with a student criterion that 'the program should give enough options and enough time for personal development'.

We may conclude that we have no yardstick at our disposal to measure the quality of education. Standards and criteria are also a matter of bargaining and negotiating between parties involved. An absolute value for the academic level or the quality of the graduates does not exist what is generally accepted as quality is a matter of opinion..

Performance indicators: a curse or a blessing for EQA?

As already said, a simplification of quality assessment is: 'define quality and look for a set of performance indicators for measuring the quality'. But the question is whether there is a real link between so-called performance indicators and quality. Opinions are divided. It is evident that, whenever people try to derive quality directly from quantitative data, differences of interpretation will arise. Consider, for example, the measurement of the quality of research. Is the total number of publications a true measure of quality? The analysis of information and experience gained elsewhere indicate that that is not always the case. Such performance indicators like the number of articles shows the danger of using performance indicators. Once set, the indicator will be corrupted as soon as possible. Instead of publishing one good article, we see now that the article is split into several articles, because each counts for the record.

Another example referring to education: the interpretation of success rates. One faculty has a pass rate of 80 per cent, another a rate of 60 per cent. But does the figure say something about the performance of the faculty? The quality of education? Is the performance of university Y with a pass rate of 80 per cent superior to the achievement of university X with a ratio of 60 per cent? Or has university Y lowered its level? Or is university X more selective in the first year?

There exists a considerable amount of literature on performance indicators (Ball and Halwachi 1987; Cave, Hanney, Kogan and

Trevet 1988; Segers, Dochy and Wijnen 1989; Goedegebuure *et al.* 1990; Dochy *et al.* 1990; Sizer 1990; Kells 1990; Spee and Bormans 1991). A striking factor in the discussion on performance indicators is that there are two opposing parties. It is mostly governments who lay a strong emphasis on the importance of using perform- ance indicators: they are optimistic about the possibility of deter- mining the right indicators. Higher education institutions, on the other hand are generally very reserved and sceptical about the use.

Many governments are trying to formulate performance indi- cators which would be useful in quality assessment, so far without any success. The following reasons can put forward:

- **The term 'performance indicator' is very confusing.** Notwithstanding the attempts to define the meaning and functions of performance indicators, the term leads to confusion. The problem is that a performance indicator is not always in direct relation to the performance of an institution, but should be considered as statistical data. Segers *et al.* (1989) formulate for example as one of the PIs the man–woman ratio in a student population. However, this indicator says nothing about the quality of an HE institution. It is more an indicator for the government indicating how far the objective 'emancipation' is realized.

- **Performance indicators have different functions.** People attach different functions to performance indicators. Without using the term 'PI', it will be clear that the use of certain data (enrolment figures, student numbers, number of graduates, unemployment figures) is important. These data play an important role in monitoring and evaluation. Governments on the other hand often look to performance indicators as an instrument for allocation. In several countries we see attempts to come to performance-based funding (Bauer 1993b; see also Section 1.8).

- **Transformation from indicators into standards.** Looking at the different functions attributed to performance indicators, it is not unreasonable to fear that indicators will be transformed into criteria. The success rates may be an indicator for realizing the goal 'to make as many students as possible graduate'. A pass rate of 70% would appear to be more successful than a pass rate of 60%. But the figure says nothing about the quality of teaching. However, there may be a tendency to specify that a success rate of at least 70% should be realized.

The conclusion should be that all attempts and all discussions of the past decade have not produced a generally accepted set of performance indicators.

Performance indicators and peer review

Is there a role for PIs in quality assessment? What is the value of performance indicators as opposed to peer review or in combination with peer review? Looking at the sets of performance indicators that have been formulated (see, for example, Segers *et al.* 1989, Sizer 1990), we can make a distinction between *quantitative* and *qualitative* indicators. The quantitative indicators are often basic data, but at once they are decorated with the notion 'PI': they concern numbers of students, numbers of staff, dropout rates, student–staff ratios. When these data are used in the right way, the 'performance' indicators will raise questions but never give an answer. The so-called qualitative performance indicators may be seen as elements which have an influence on the quality aspects to be taken into account when looking at the quality. The question is whether we can (or will) rely more on the performance indicators than on the subjective judgements of peers.

The role of performance indicators in quality assessment is a limited one as can be illustrated with the following example:

> I have a bottle of wine and want to assess its quality. Which aspects are important? First I have to decide on which aspects I will assess the wine: acidity, tannin, alcohol percentage, sediment. Of course I can measure these wine on this aspects, but still I do not know whether the wine is good or not. Someone has to tell which figure is good and which one not. But there are other aspects more important for the assessment: taste and smell. These aspects are not quantifiable. We need a panel that can judge the taste and smell as fine or not. (Vroeijenstijn 1993b; see Figure 1.2)

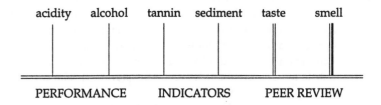

Figure 1.2. *The relationship between performance indicators and peer review*

As an intermezzo here is an example of how misleading the use of performance indicators may be. In the middle of 1989 Dutch papers published a lot of reactions and commentaries on the report of the ministerial Reconnaissance Committee for Theology (Verkenningscommissie Godgeleerdheid 1989). The quality of the faculties of Theology at Dutch universities was poor. Not a single faculty reached the international level. The committee said to have looked at Theology through several 'windows' or 'spectacles' as the committee called the indicators: productivity, qualifications of the staff, number of theses, number of young researchers, assessment of research programmes by external bodies, editorship of scientific journals.

For the productivity index the committee set a standard of one book every five years and one article every year for a full-time appointment. As international standard the committee set one book every four years and two articles yearly. Based on the counting of publications and weighing them with points (a book in the Dutch language 10 points, in a foreign language 15 points; a Dutch article 1 point, and in a foreign language 3 points), the committee ranked the faculties and derived conclusions about the scientific level. The conclusion was that not one faculty reached the international standard, and only two reached the national one.

However, the standard and the awarding of points are based on arbitrary decisions. Why is a Dutch book worth 10 points and a foreign book 15 instead of 4 and 8 points, respectively, as another ministerial committee for Educational Science and Pedagogics had given (Visitatiecommissie Pedagogiek en Onderwijskunde 1987)?

Why one book every five years instead of one in six or four years? Why are ten Dutch articles equal to a book in the Dutch language but you have to write only five articles in a foreign language to get the same points as a book in a foreign language? Recalculation with other weights and standards changes the outcome. With regard to the scientific level, more faculties reach the standard. The conclusion is that, working with arbitrary weights and standards, the outcome must be handled very carefully. A major objection lies in the way the figures are used with a degree of absoluteness. The figures are no longer indicators but become criteria. Reading the report one gets the impression that the committee has viewed Theology in the Netherlands through several windows, but did not enter the building to ask questions. So far as is traceable in the report, the committee did not look at the quality of the publications, nor did it ask questions about why and how. The committee looked at the scientific work of the Theological faculties with seven different pairs of spectacles on. Depending on the number of spectacles the committee put on, the picture for some faculties became blacker and blacker.

Working with performance indicators is so attractive because we may get a clear picture of strong points and weak spots. But these analyses must be handled very carefully and complemented with other information. The conclusion is that PIs play some role in quality assessment, but only a minor one. Performance indicators in the broad sense (that is to say qualitative and quantitative indicators) are the point of departure for getting quality in the picture. Performance indicators in a narrow sense (the set of quantitative performance indicators) play a role in supporting the opinion of peers. But performance indicators can never have the last say or take the place of peer review. The opinion of peers must be based on facts and figures, but can never be replaced by performance indicators. 'Performance indicators should be used not as an end in themselves to draw definitive conclusions, but to trigger areas of concern and provide a catalyst for further investigation' (Ashworth and Harvey 1994). It will be clear that performance indicators can never speak for themselves, but must be interpreted by experts. Where they seem to be objective, they are not really performance indicators, but only statistical data or management information. Just as is the case regarding the concept 'quality', it is also a waste of time searching for the philosopher's stone: a set of performance indicators to measure quality.

1.6 Institutional or Programme Review?

When designing a system for EQA, several decisions have to be made. One of these is deciding at what level the assessment will be done. This depends on the purpose. Is it wanted for institutional accreditation? Is it required for checking the way quality is assured? Or do we want to penetrate deeper into the organisation and aim at feedback on the curriculum or the research programme by experts? It will be clear that every choice will have its own advantages and disadvantages.

Examples of institution-wide assessment are the approach by the Higher Education Quality Council (HEQC) in the UK and the approach by the Comité National d'Evaluation in France.

The HEQC describes the purpose as:

> to review and verify the effectiveness of an institution's systems and procedures for assuring the quality of its teaching and learning. Quality audit does not seek to assess or to evaluate the validity of an institution's mission or objectives *per se*, or the appropriateness of the desired outcomes. It will, however, seek to review and comment upon procedures for quality assurance, and their operation in practice, against an institution's stated objectives. (HEQC 1993)

Advantages of the system are that it asks for fewer experts, is less time consuming and less expensive. It is a check on the quality procedures in an institution.

The approach of the CNE in France differs from that of the HEQC. The CNE quality assessment procedure consists of two parts: institution-wide evaluations and sometimes 'horizontal', disciplinary reviews. The institutional evaluations are not specific down to the individual level, nor do they assess courses (Staropoli 1992, Ottenwaelter 1993). In contrast to the HEQC approach, the CNE looks not only at the way quality is assured, but also tries to assess the quality of the institute and its components.

A disadvantage of the institutional approach is that there will be little involvement at grass-roots level, no feedback at discipline level, no recommendations for improvement of the curriculum.

The involvement of the individual staff member will be low and advice on improvement of the programme rare. This will be compensated for by the discipline reviews.

In truth, the heading of this section is not quite correct. The choice is not between institutional and programme review, but *both* institutional and programme review. In Figure 1.3 the relation between the three levels institutional audit, faculty assessment and programme assessment is given.

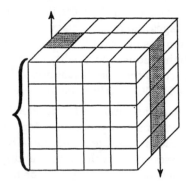

Programme assessment (teaching and/or research)
- content analysis
- feedback to grassroot level

Institutional audit
- accreditation
- crowning stone
- feedback for management

Faculty assessment
- combination of audit and assessment
- feedback for management and grass root level

Figure 1.3. The relationship between institutional audit, faculty assessment and programme assessment

Institutional audit

Institutional audit can be done for the sake of accreditation. In that case a light assessment procedure may be used. The minimum requirements or standards will be formulated outside the institution. In some cases it will be possible to take into account past performance, but mostly people will look at conditions for being a real higher education institution. Given the boundary conditions, may we expect quality from that institution for higher education institution? In this light, important aspects to be assessed are:

- the mission statement. Does it fit in with the expected values of higher education?
- staffing and the qualifications of the staff
- number of faculties and the variety of programmes offered
- facilities
- the internal quality assurance mechanism.

When accreditation is not the direct purpose, an institutional assessment should be considered as the keystone of the programme-oriented EQA system. Starting with programme assessment or departmental assessment, once in the cycle the institution as a whole should be assessed too. The institutional assessment should be done at the end of a cycle of programme assessments. The outcomes of the programme assessments can be used during the institutional assessment and can be connected with the findings of the institutional audit. All findings can be coupled. This institutional assessment will also be based on self-assessment and external assessment. The topics for the self-assessment and for discussion with the external committee are:

- the mission and profile of the institution
- central policy regarding education and research
- organisation and management
- central facilities, like library, educational support
- funding system
- internal quality assurance mechanism.

Faculty or departmental assessment

There can be three reasons for having faculty assessment instead of a single programme assessment:

1. Sometimes a programme assessment will coincide with a faculty assessment, for example in the case of the assessment of Law in the Netherlands. There is such a affinity between the programmes offered that all programmes in the faculty of Law will be assessed. The same is the case for Economics.
2. Sometimes the relationship is looser, but the faculty board would like to know more about the connections.

3. On other occasions single programme assessments will cause problems assessing a very segmented faculty, for example Humanities or Social Sciences. A programme assessment overtaxes the faculty. It is always busy with assessment; one committee is leaving while the other is arriving. Another disadvantage is that a committee pays attention only to the individual programme and not to the connections between the programmes, the profile of the faculty and the contribution of all segments to the realisation of the profile.

The first two possibilities do not cause problems. The same method as described in this book can be used. For the third case, assessment of a segmented faculty, an adaptation should be made. However, it will be clear that an assessment of a faculty with many programmes will lose some of the advantages of a programme assessment. It will be more an assessment of boundary conditions than an assessment of the (content of a) programme. The feedback will be more towards policy-makers and administrators than towards staff and students.

In Appendix 6 an adapted version for faculty assessment is given. There is as yet no real experience of this way of assessment, but it looks as though it will be feasible for faculties such as Liberal Arts or Humanities.

Programme assessment

At the other end of the scale stands the assessment of the curricula: a review committee will assess a curriculum or several curricula in a cognate domain. This approach offers the opportunity to go into depth and details. It will involve the individual staff members and the committee may give feedback and recommendations for the enhancement of the quality of the curriculum.

However, there are several disadvantages too: it is time-consuming and more expensive. In some faculties with many curricula, like Humanities, this approach may lead towards almost continuous assessment: one committee is leaving as the next is arriving. While most faculties in the Netherlands will be visited once or maybe twice in a six-year period (for example faculty of Economic Sciences, faculty of Law), the faculty of Humanities (which includes programmes like history, languages, liberal arts, etc.) has been visited nearly every year since the start of external quality assessment in Dutch universities in 1988. In such a case, another solution should be looked for, keeping the values of a content approach but diminishing the burden.

Because quality is primarily determined by what happens in a faculty, especially in the teaching/learning situation, the best way to start with external quality assessment is to start with assessing programmes in a specific domain. But of course, it is all very well to assess quality on department level, but what about the contribution of central services and the institution as a whole? Therefore, it will be necessary to complete programme reviews with a review of central services and general management.

1.7 Teaching/Learning and Research in Tandem?

As already said in the Preface, this book is more about the assessment of teaching and learning than about assessing research. One of the reasons is that the assessment of research already has a long tradition. Researchers are already accustomed to being assessed by colleagues. The quality of research output is assessed, for example, by assessing publications in refereed journals. Researchers are meeting each other at conferences and discussing each other's research work. Research councils are assessing proposals before they allow grants. For research there is already an open (inter)national scholarly community assessing each other's activities. Such a scholarly community for teaching and learning did not exist. Thinking about the design of an EQA system, there will arise the question of whether it is possible and desirable to combine the assessment of the learning/teaching process and the assessment of research.

The policy in the Netherlands is to start with external quality assessment of teaching, excluding research. This has been decided upon for two reasons: first, combining research and teaching would mean that teaching loses out once more; secondly there already existed an assessment system of research by research councils. In 1993 the VSNU started a separate system for assessment of research, based on the same principles as the assessment of teaching (VSNU 1993b). For a short description of the system see Appendix 7.

There are other reasons for a separate approach: the expertise necessary for the assessment of research is different from the expertise for the assessment of teaching/learning. For research you need peers, specialists in the research field to be assessed; for education you need experts with a broad overview over the discipline. But there are very practical reasons too: combining assessment of research projects and research programmes with the education programme review requires very big committees. Also the amount of time for a visit to the faculty would be much longer.

But of course, the link between teaching and research is characteristic of a university. This means that the educational quality cannot be assessed without taking into account this link. There are questions which cannot be avoided and must be answered during the assessment, such as: in which way do students come into contact with research? What role does research play in the programme? How are the most recent developments in the field of research reflected in the curriculum? But the assessment of research projects or research programmes are no part of the terms of reference of a committee assessing teaching. Therefore, the best way is to assess teaching and research separately, although it will be useful if each assessment is planned with the other in mind.

1.8 The Connection with Funding

Looking at the Dutch 'model' for EQA and for example the British 'model' (see Stubbs 1994), we see as one of the striking differences the link with funding. In the UK there is a direct connection: quality assessment is a task of the funding councils and the outcomes influence a part of the funding. In the Netherlands the connection is indirect: the outcomes will influence the funding in the long run. In practice the government may stop the funding of a programme when a prolonged lack of quality has been determined. For example: a committee of experts judges the quality of programme Y as unsatisfactory. The faculty will get time to improve it. After six years (or maybe shorter if the situation is really bad), the next committee will investigate what has been done with the recommendations. If the situation is still bad, the minister can warn the faculty and announce his intention to stop the funding. Then there is still time for the faculty to give notice of appeal, before the real decision is made.

The discussion is not whether there should be a link between quality and funding. Of course there is and will be. The question is what this link should be. In my opinion there are only two reasons to have a direct link. The first reason is, of course, when the assessment is done for accreditation. The second reason is to connect a part of the funding with the condition that an institution participate in one way or another in external quality assessment. In all other cases, a direct link between funding and outcomes of the assessment is pernicious. Van Vught expressed it in this way: 'To try to relate a system of rewards and sanctions to the delicate mechanism of quality assessment is the best way to make sure that the quality assessment system will not work. Creating a relationship between quality assessment and funding, will almost certainly lead to a compliance culture' (1991).

Also the Liaison Committee of Rectors' Conferences advises that the link between quality assessment and funding decisions should be indirect (Liaison Committee 1993). But, after the first ghost of performance indicators, we see now a second ghost walking through governmental Europe. It is no longer only the British government that is charmed by the direct link and a performance-based funding. More governments now like to link a certain percentage of the budget directly with the outcomes of assessment: Denmark and Sweden are examples of this way of thinking (Bauer 1993). Behind the idea of earmarking money for quality still lies the optimistic idea that it is possible to steer higher education centrally. Another problem with performance-based funding is that it is often aiming at rewarding excellence or promoting excellence. But why should we award extra money to the already excellent faculties? Why not use the money to strengthen weak quality?

1.9 Horizontal and Comparative Approach

Another choice to be made when designing a system for EQA is about the scope of the assessment. Will the external assessment team visit several institutions (a horizontal and comparative approach) or only one? The principles and recommendations laid down in this book can be used for external quality assessment of more than one institute by the same committee. However they can be applied also for the assessment of only one faculty, school, department or curriculum. The difference lies in the way of reporting.

In several countries (the Netherlands, Denmark, Portugal) the choice has been made to carry out the assessment nationwide. That is, one committee will assess the same programme in all institutions. Of course this is only possible when there are not too many institutions. Experience shows that about 10 visits is the maximum you may ask from a committee. But of course, when there are more units to be assessed, it will be possible to combine a number of them and organize the assessment on a regional basis.

There are several reasons for organizing the assessment in a horizontal and comparative way:

- External quality assessment also has a public function, so there will be a request for a comparative approach. Although not aiming for ranking or formulating league tables, there will be a question of how quality aspects of one faculty compare with the same aspects in other faculties. The government wants insight into the quality of the programmes both for the incoming students and for employers. This can only be done when all programmes or groups of programmes are assessed by the same committee.

- However, it is not only the government that will pay attention to the comparison. The institutions themselves are interested, too. They like to know their own position in the field.

- A horizontal approach also has a meaning for the subject area involved. By assessing more programmes, a committee may get a good picture of the state of the art in the subject area and sketch future developments in favour of the faculties involved.

- The assessment of more programmes by the same committee also promotes equal treatment of the faculties concerned. In particular, when the reports are public, it will be important that faculties are treated and assessed in more or less the same way.

- Although a separate assessment of a programme seems to be less expensive and less time-consuming for the members of a committee, there will certainly be a problem of finding experts for every separate assessment. It will be more effective to do the assessment as a joint effort.

1.10 Government and Higher Education Institutions: Opponents or Allies in EQA?

There are many players in the game 'quality assessment' and it is not always easy to satisfy every player, because the expectations are not always the same. The players in the field are (see Figure 1.4): the higher education institutions, the deans of departments, schools and faculties, the staff responsible for the curricula, the students, the government, an inspectorate, the parliament. Everybody emphasizes the need to guarantee quality because quality is the concern of all parties. However, the question is: who is responsible for quality assurance?

Looking at the developments in different countries, we cannot say that the higher education institutions on the one side and the government on the other side have joined hands to tackle the problem of quality and quality assurance. We cannot always call

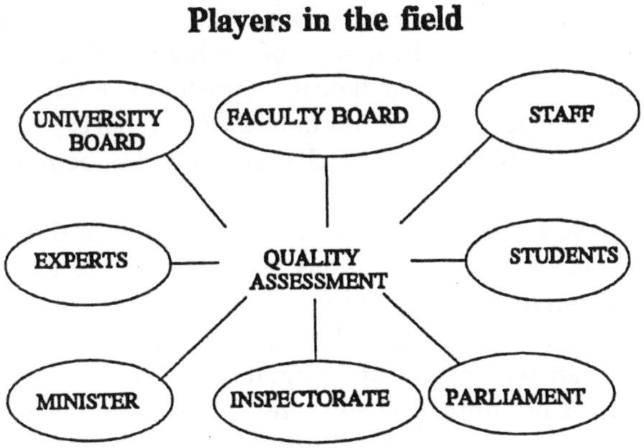

Players in the field

Figure 1.4. Players in the game of quality assessment

them friends and allies. On the contrary, it is often a duel. Who is doing what and why?
With regard to the following topics governments and higher education institutions may have different opinions:

- the purpose of quality assessment
- the responsibility for the assessment: who does what?

- the possibility of defining quality
- the use of performance indicators
- the link with funding
- the effects of EQA.

Governments and higher education institutions are in most countries still opponents as regards the 'why' of external quality assessment. As already said, governments often have a very simplistic idea about quality and quality assessment. They think that it is easy to define quality and to measure it. Maybe they will always stay opponents, because the gap between the two sides is widest in the interpretation of the concept of quality. Quality requirements set by governments may really be threatening for the quality of higher education. For the different views on the definition of quality see Section 1.4; for the use of performance indicators see Section 1.5; for the link with funding see Section 1.8.

Governments also often have a very simplistic idea about the effects of quality assessment. They assume that EQA will have direct consequences for the quality of the higher education institutions, that there is an immediate response following the findings and recommendations of the committees of external experts: if the assessment takes place in year x, changes should be demonstrable in year $x+1$.

There have passed five years of intensive EQA in the Netherlands. An outsider will ask whether the quality of the universities really has been improved. If universities stress that improvement is the main function of EQA, will it be possible to show that it really works? The answer is disappointing: the quality of Dutch higher education has not improved substantially. After an investigation into the effects of EQA, carried out by order of the Minister of Education and Science, the researchers conclude: 'However, we cannot say that the large amount of resources invested immediately leads to an equally large improvement of the quality of education: measures are not taken in response to every recommendation, nor are the measures taken drastic measures' (Frederiks, Westerheijden and Weusthof 1993). This conclusion is not unexpected or inexplicable, but we do not need to conclude that it is better to stop the time- and money-consuming activity of EQA, because 'the effects of a "quality culture" cannot and should not be expected to be immediate and large. Quality of Education, however important, is only one of a multitude of issues in the institutions for higher education; it will take time to grow above the level of the roots it is putting out now; less far-reaching measures may have large effects in future years' (Frederiks *et al.* 1993). The report contains a warning for governments not to think too simplistically about the effects and follow-up. Innovations and changes will take time and there will never be a direct, short-term link between the activities in the field of quality assessment and improvement. But in general we may conclude that a lot is happening in the faculties, in a direct or indirect way, as a result of the external quality assessment. The mere existence of the system already affects the way of thinking about quality in the university. Over the five years in the Netherlands quality awareness has been increased. Quality is on the agenda, teaching has gained ground. Perhaps the most important effect of EQA can be described as 'promoting the quality debate'.

1.11 Between the Scylla of Improvement and the Charybdis of Accountability

External quality assessment has two purposes: quality improvement and accountability. To fulfil these two purposes, managing the EQA-process, is like navigating between two extremes. When one aims only at improvement, the system will be shipwrecked against the 'Scylla' because the outside stakeholders will ask for accountability and design their own EQA system. If accountability is emphasised too much, the system will disappear in the 'Charybdis', because improvement will be hindered or even made impossible. The challenge is to keep on course and, by doing so, reconcile the two purposes in one system. It will be not easy, as can be seen by looking at the experience of the Netherlands.

In April 1986 the minister and the higher education institutions agreed that EQA was the responsibility of the higher education institutions themselves. Inevitably, an agreement between two parties always causes interpretation problems. The debate during the past five years has focused in particular on the aims of quality assessment and on what might be expected from quality control. The government has formulated the following aims for the EQA:

- **To improve teaching and learning.**
- **To promote accountability:** 'The institutions of HE can shape thee responsibility towards the society with the help of the outcomes of the quality assessment. This is supplementary to the enlarged autonomy. This function is seen as important because HE can render an account on the quality of education and research to the parliament, based on the outcomes of the assessment' (Ministerie van Onderwijs en Wetenschappen 1990).
- **To contribute to the planning procedures.** Differences in quality become visible. This can play a role in the discussion on the development of higher education.
- **To inform society** about the state of the art of HE. For example, information for prospective students about the quality of the programmes offered at the different institutions and about prospects for the labour market (Ministerie van Onderwijs en Wetenschappen 1990).

With the last aim in mind, we may point to the importance the Dutch government attaches to the role of students in the framework of quality assessment. The Dutch Minister for Education and Science has taken the initiative of publishing a book for students as a tool for the evaluation of their education. It stresses the role they can play in quality assessment. The Minister also subsidized the publication of a periodical, the *Consumer Guide for Higher Education* (*Kenzegids Hoger Onderwijs 1992–1994*). It attempts to describe the quality of the different study programmes in a comparative way. The idea behind the *Guide* is the belief that, when students have enough information at their disposal, they will choose their study on the basis of quality and by doing so will vote with their feet and force the higher education institutions to deliver good quality education.

There is no difference in opinion between universities and the government about the aim 'quality improvement'. Quality assessment is first and foremost aimed at discovering weaknesses and at enhancing and improving quality.

The interpretation of the aim 'accountability' however has caused a lot of discussion. The question is what is accountability all about? In the opinion of the universities, they render an account of their performance in the annual reports. The reports of the external assessment should not be burdened with general account-ability of money spent and efficiency. Accountability in the frame-work of EQA should be related exclusively to the way universities handle quality and quality assurance. In that respect the review committee also plays a role.

For the universities, an important role of EQA is to contribute to *self-regulation*. Until 1985, the government often sought to steer higher education by detailed interference and state regulation. The new philosophy of greater autonomy means that the universities themselves investigate whether their goals and aims are realized and whether the process of realizing the goals and aims is under control. This self-regulation should increasingly take the place of state regulation. Self-regulation must be based on a good system of quality assessment and quality assurance.

Kells (1992, 1993) gives the following definition or set of attrib-utes for a self-regulating university. Such a university:

- reviews regularly its university and programme level stated intentions (purposes, goals, objectives) for clarity, completeness, consensus, interrelatedness and achievement

- assigns firm responsibility to a person or office for evaluation, for implementing the results, for follow-up, and for links to budgets and plans

- builds an active, useful, evolving information system containing both facts and opinions about its programmes and services. It listens to clients and it expects leaders and staff members to use such information

- reviews itself on a schedule that makes sense (programmes, services and management) using self-assessment *processes* and then peer reviews to validate the results. It periodically also looks at the whole university – its policies, strategies and directions

- acts on results of reviews: uses incentives and sanctions; redistributes marginal resources – even deletes a service or programme now and then.

Universities stress improvement as the main purpose of EQA and all other aims as subordinate to it. A committee of experts is not a supplier of information for the government nor a cheap inspec-torate, but a mirror and a sounding-board for the faculty. But as far as possible EQA shall play also a public role, although the accountability side not should be overemphasised.

1.12 Basic Principles for a System of EQA

The design of an EQA system depends on the purposes one has in mind. In Section 1.3 we explained that it will not always be necessary to set up a separate EQA system for realizing these purposes. The best way is to design an EQA system aiming at quality enhancement and as side-effects (partial) accountability. For the design of the system, some basic principles may be formulated.

1. It must be clear to all parties concerned (government, parliament, higher education institutes – staff and students) what may be expected from EQA

There are several reasons for deciding on EQA, as became clear in Section 1.3. Expectations regarding the purposes and the outcomes of EQA may differ between governments and universities. Do we choose a quality control system for measuring quality (as far as that is possible)? Do we wish to use the system for allocation of funds? Or are we planning the system as an instrument for quality maintenance and enhancement? All those possible purposes are legitimate. But it must be clear to all parties concerned what the aim is. It does not make sense to stress the improvement function, but use the outcomes for allocation or reallocation of money without warning the higher education institutions that this will be done.

The choice 'controlling and measuring', which is often wanted by governments, is legitimate, but do not expect too much cooperation by the higher education institutions. Nobody likes to provide the rope to be hanged with.

2. Do not overcharge the system of EQA with summative and formative functions. It is hard for EQA to serve two masters

While in the formulation of the purpose of EQA it is important to try to combine the expectations of the higher education institutions and the wishes of the outside world, it will be necessary to keep in mind that quality will benefit more from the improvement approaches than from control. Therefore it is important not to burden the system too much with accountability and information delivering.

It may be difficult for an improvement-oriented system of EQA to realize at the same time a public function. It will be far more difficult and maybe impossible for an accountability-based system to contribute to quality enhancement.

3. EQA does not aim at ranking and is not directly connected with funding

There is nowadays a tendency to publish league tables or 'Top-10' lists of higher education institutions or faculties. External quality assessment will have a certain comparative aspect when more faculties are involved, but it must be clearly stated that a comparison of quality aspects does not mean ranking and is not aiming at it. Ranking is inappropriate because adding the assessment of the distinguishing aspects does not make sense; the detailed assessment will lose all meaning. If ranking is to be connected with EQA, it will be a threat to improvement, because the faculty will show only its strengths and not its bad points. The same applies to a direct connection with funding.

4. Quality is foremost the responsibility of the higher education institutions. Therefore they must have the 'ownership' of the system of EQA

This is one of the cardinal principles: it is the higher education institutions themselves which are responsible for quality and so for quality assurance. Quality improvement starts at institutional level and can never be forced upon a department. EQA should never be an instrument in the hands of a government, but should be an instrument in the hands of the higher education institutions, the faculty, department or school, in the hands of the staff. For that reason the higher education institutions should be made responsible for the design and maintenance of the system. Therefore:

5. Higher education institutions will be set up an umbrella organisation responsible for the coordination and execution of EQA

The setting up and maintaining of an EQA system require coordination by an inter-institutional organisation or an umbrella organisation, like the Association of Universities in the Netherlands (VSNU). This body can be formed by the higher education institutions with the mission to organise the EQA.

6. A body outside the higher education institutions will be made responsible for the evaluation of the assessment, also called meta-evaluation, preventing degeneration of the system and in-breeding

Because the higher education institutions are the owners of the system, there should be an outside body as watchdog, keeping the system transparent, honest and reliable. That authority will assess the assessment, also called meta-evaluation. This meta-evaluative role can be performed by an independent body like an Inspectorate, but can also be done by the minister. This issue will be considered further in Section 2.8.

7. EQA is never an end in itself, but is complementary to internal quality assurance

It does not make sense to build a system for EQA without connection with internal quality assurance. EQA has to be seen as one of the instruments in the hands of the faculty. This issue will be considered further in Section 2.3.

8. The basic elements of the EQA system are (a) self-assessment and (b) peer review

An EQA system may never be based on performance indicators alone. It may never be based on paperwork only. The cornerstone of the system is a self-assessment by the unit under review (see Section 2.4). The second element is the peer review, 'holding a mirror' to the unit (see Section 2.5).

9. EQA must be regular and cyclical

It does not make sense to have a unique assessment. EQA must be done on a regular basis. One of the strengths of the system is the ability to look at improvements after a certain period of time. The next committee will ask what has been done with the recommendations of the preceding committee.

10. EQA must result in a report

Every external assessment will end with a report. There may be a discussion about confidentiality or not. So far as it concerns the accountability, the outcomes will be published. Government and higher education institutions must agree about the aspects to be treated. The report will play an important role in the balance between improvement and accountability.

11. Governments must abstain from direct actions based on the outcomes and leave the follow-up to the higher education institutions

Of course, government will watch Argus-eyed the outcomes of an assessment. It will not always be easy for it to keep itself at a distance and not to interfere. It has, however, in the first instance to be left to the higher education institutions to take actions and to do something with it. Only when an institution does nothing with the recommendations may the minister carpet the institution. If the minister takes measures at too early a stage, it will probably mean the end of the system, because no institution will cooperate and have an open dialogue with a committee in future. But of course, government likes to know whether EQA has some effect or not. Therefore the following principle:

12. The higher education institutions will give a clear statement in the annual report about what they have done or are planning to do with the recommendations

Innovations and changes take time. Therefore it will not always be easy to show the outside world that quality is improving on a large scale. An institution should at least report to the outside world what it thinks about the recommendations of a committee and what it will do with them.

13. *Higher education institutions will be safeguarded against external quality assessment by different bodies or authorities*

Higher education institutions are subjected to several assessments. Sometimes higher education is squeezed to death by all the attention focused on quality. In some cases faculties are more talking about quality than supplying quality, because there is no time to do anything with all the remarks and recommendations. Therefore, it is advisable to be very economical with external quality assessment. If there does exist for example an assessment by a professional body and an assessment by a funding council, people should strive for an agreement to use the outcomes of one assessment for the planned second assessment.

14. *Cost–benefit*

Last but not least, it will be clear that the system should be cost effective. We have to make a distinction between the cost of a faculty/school preparing itself for the external assessment by carrying out the self-assessment and the cost of the review committee. Because most faculties/schools do not have a tradition of self-assessment, the first time will be time-consuming. The better the internal quality management, all the easier will be the self-assessment. The first time, a faculty may need about six months for the self-assessment; the second time it should be possible to do it in one month.

The second item for the cost is the cost of the assessment agency. This expense depends on the size of the committees, the number of faculties to be visited etc.

The cost–benefit will be defined by the value of the recommendations by the experts. The recommendations should link up with the experiences and needs of the faculty. It will be the task of EQA to minimize the costs and efforts and to maximize the benefits.

1.13 Concluding Remarks

Before an effective EQA system can be designed, certain decisions have to be made. When doing so, keep the following in mind:

- Do not try to discover a definition of quality. It is a waste of time. However, every party concerned (students, staff, government, employers) should make clear what its requirements are.

- Avoid a discussion about performance indicators. That is also a waste of time.
- Be very clear about the purpose of quality assessment. A good agreement between the higher education institutions and the government about responsibilities should be made.
- A system for EQA is based on self-assessment, peer review and site visits.

Chapter Two

Designing an EQA System

This chapter is based on the experience of six years of external quality assessment in Dutch universities. In a way it gives a description of the Dutch approach. At the same time an attempt is made to generalize the ideas into an example design of an EQA system. The basic principles treated in Chapter 1 are applied. However, readers need to adapt the given design to this national context, as far as possible adhering to the basic principles.

The design of an effective EQA system starts with the decision to place the responsibility for it in the hands of the higher education institutions. The most vital purpose is contributing to quality maintenance and quality enhancement. However, the system will have a public function too. Therefore the formulation of the aims might be:

> The aim of EQA is primarily *to contribute to quality maintenance and, where necessary, to quality improvement*. A derived aim is *to provide a good view of the quality of education and/or research*. The recommendations for quality improvement and the insight into quality must lead to action, that is, *self-regulation*.

In this formulation it is clear that 'quality improvement' is the main objective of all efforts. The aim: 'to provide a good view of the quality of education and/or research' summarizes the governmental aims 'accountability' and 'providing information'.

In this chapter the following topics will be discussed:

- The role of the assessment agency
- How to convince the faculties
- Internal quality care as a condition for EQA
- Self-assessment: cornerstone of EQA
- The review committee

- The report of the review committee
- The follow-up
- Who guards the guardians?
- Students and quality assessment.

For guidelines for self-assessment see Chapter 3; for guidelines for the review committee see Chapter 4.

2.1 The Role of the Assessment Agency

Once the decision is made about the responsibility for the EQA system and government and higher education institutions have agreed on the broad outlines, it is important to set up a bureau or an agency for working out the system and the daily activities regarding the assessment. Because the assessment is the responsibility of the higher education institutions, this agency will work independently from government. But it is also desirable that the agency can act, within the framework set by the higher education institutions, independently of the institutions, protecting EQA from the whims of the institutions and the whims of the government.

How many staff are needed? The Association of Universities in the Netherlands (the VSNU) is responsible for the assessment of teaching and research in 14 universities. For the EQA in full practice there is the following staffing:

- General coordination: 0.6 FTE (full-time equivalents)
- For the management of EQA 'teaching': 0.5 FTE
- For the management of EQA 'research': 0.5 FTE
- For the secretariat of the review committees for teaching/learning: 3.0 FTE (about six committees yearly)
- for the assessment committees for research: 3.0 FTE (about six committees yearly)
- Support by administrative staff: 2.0 FTE.

To start with, you need a coordinator and a secretary for each committee that will be run.

What is the cost of the system? This is difficult to say because a part of the cost depends on expenses for travelling and lodging. It depends also on how much experts will be paid. To give an

impression, figures for six years' assessment in the Dutch universities are given. In the past six years, 28 committees have assessed
328 programmes during 163 visits; 242 experts have been involved.
Counting together the time the members have spent, they have
worked 70 years full time. The VSNU have spent about 2.8 million
ECU. The experts did not get a fee. If we had paid the normal expert
tariff, it would have cost another 7 million ECU. An estimate shows
that the universities together have spent about 10 million ECU on
self-assessment and on preparation for the visits. A calculation
shows that universities are spending about 0.4% of the total budget
for education on self-assessment, preparation for the committees
and the visits. Per student we are spending 3 ECU at VSNU level
and about 10 ECU at university level (Table 2.1).

Table 2.1. Figures with Regard to EQA at the Dutch Universities in the Period 1988–1993

Number of committees	28
Number of experts involved	242
Number of visits	163
Number of assessed programmes	328
Total time spent by committee members	70 years
Total expenses in 6 years	2.8 million ECU
If we had paid the normal expert tariff	7 million ECU
Expenses VSNU + expenses of the universities in 6 years	13 million ECU
Total expenses as % of the budget for education	0.4%
Cost per student per year	13 ECU

The role of the agency concerns:

- information and guidance for the self-assessment
- composing the review committees
- instructing and training of the committees
- training and counselling of the secretaries
- organising the visits and backing the process

- publishing the report
- dialogue with the minister and the authority for meta-evaluation.

Most of the activities of the agency are in the preparatory phase. The assessment agency will also explain to the faculties to be assessed how the self-assessment should be done and the purpose of it. Therefore the guidelines for the self-assessment can be used (see Chapter 3). The agency will also be in charge of the training of the committees and the secretaries. For that purpose the guidelines for the review committee in Chapter 4 can be used.

In Table 2.2 the schedule of the activities of the agency is given.

Table 2.2. Schedule of the Activities of the Assessment Agency

One year before the review (= X)	Formal letter to the institutions with the announcement of the review
Same time	Letter to the deans of the faculties asking for nomination of committee members
	Looking for the members
X + 2 months	Nomination of the committee to the board of the Association. If agreed upon the select list, approach chairman and members
In the period X up to X + 6	Workshops for the units involved
	Units to be assessed carry out the self-assessment
3 months before first meeting of the committee	The units to be assessed present the self-assessments to the agency
	Agency plans the reviews in consultation with the committee
One year after the formal announcement (= Y)	First meeting of the committee: training and introduction
Y + maximum 6 months	Visits to the units to be assessed
3 months after last visit	Publication of the report
	Discharge of the committee

During the visits, the agency has nothing or very little to do with the process. The committees act independently, although the agency keeps an eye on the process from a distance. Only in the final stages (the publication of the report) does the agency come back into the picture.

2.2 How to Convince the Faculties/Departments

Decisions about EQA will often be made at the central level of the higher education institutions. It will be the Presidents, the Chancellors, Vice-Chancellors or Rectors who will negotiate with the Minister about the EQA. For the staff and students in faculties, departments or schools it will be something at a distance. Therefore the first mission of the agency will be the organisation of seminars for the faculties to instruct them about the why and how.

The most effective way is to organise a half-day workshop in a higher education institution, explaining the background and the system. In doing so, the workshop leader will regularly meet certain questions:

- What are the reasons for external quality assessment?
- Why additional work, when we already pay attention to quality?
- What will be done with the outcome? Are we putting forward the fibres for the rope with which we will be hanged?
- What will be the effect of external quality assessment on the faculties?

WHY EXTERNAL QUALITY ASSESSMENT?

Relating to the review committees we have heard in Dutch faculties the following opinions:

- The review committees are forced upon the higher education institutions by the Minister of Education and Science.
- It was a very smart move by the Minister of Education and Science to ask the higher education institutions to set up a system for external quality assessment; in this way he has at his disposal a low-cost inspectorate.

The faculties also sometimes say that the committees are forced upon them by the Executive Board of the university, because the joint higher education institutions agreed with the minister to take the external quality assessment in their own hands.

In a negative way one may say that the EQA is forced upon the higher education institutions by the changing attitude of many governments. Thinking positively, one may say that autonomy asks for assurance of quality: no freedom of programming, no autonomy without accountability and quality assessment. Higher education institutions have the choice of taking the responsibility for it or leaving it to an inspectorate or the minister. Autonomy and assurance of quality are the two sides of one coin.

WHY ADDITIONAL WORK, WHEN WE ALREADY PAY ATTENTION TO QUALITY?

Faculties will complain that they already pay attention to quality: why ask for more? It cannot be denied that for higher education quality has always been a key word; now though, quality assessment and evaluation has become a more public matter. There has been a lot of experience with (often *ad hoc*) evaluation; however, there is little tradition of real self-assessment.

During the first five years of EQA in the Netherlands, it appeared that the self-assessment was felt by the faculties as the most important part of the whole process (Frederiks *et al.* 1993). It must be made very clear that, first time around, the self-assessment will require a great deal of effort, but that once having established a good system of internal quality care, with data-collection procedures in place, the effort required will be far less. It should also be stressed that the self-assessment can replace other activities: e.g. in the year of the self-assessment, the unit may not need to deliver the annual report. However, the annual report can never replace the self-assessment report.

WHAT WILL BE DONE WITH THE OUTCOME? ARE WE PUTTING FORWARD THE FIBRES FOR THE ROPE WITH WHICH WE WILL BE HANGED?

Another question from the side of the faculties with regard to EQA will be 'What will be done with the outcome?' This is a fair question, especially given that the start of the system of external quality assessment in the Netherlands did not take place under the most favourable conditions. In 1986 the Minister of Education and Science had established ministerial visiting committees for some disciplines within the framework of selective retrenchment and task reallocation. There was a direct link between the outcome and closure of some departments.

Success or failure of the system of quality assessment depends not only on the willingness of higher education institutions and faculties to cooperate and take it seriously, but also on the way minister and inspectorate handle the outcome. It is necessary for them to stay in the background, watching if and how the institutions ensure quality. They must not interfere directly on the basis of the outcome, but must give the higher education institutions five to ten years to establish a system which functions properly.

WHAT IS THE EFFECT OF EXTERNAL QUALITY ASSESSMENT ON THE FACULTIES?

Speaking about the effects of external quality assessment on the faculties we must make a distinction between effects before and effects after the visit.

One of the purposes of external quality assessment is to stimulate the attention paid to quality. We can state that the planned visit of the committee already has an impact on the faculty. Knowing that the committee is going to come stimulates reflection on the teaching and learning process. Another effect of external quality assessment is that in several higher education institutions the central level has set up an internal system of quality assessment, covering all faculties. Sometimes, too, we feel that a faculty will use a review committee as a sounding-board for innovations of the curriculum.

When the review committee has visited the faculty it is possible that the faculty closes the door and says 'that was that' and proceed with the order of the day. That sometimes happens, but is not common. The review committee has made recommendations and the faculties will usually do something with the results.

2.3 Internal Quality Care

Quality maintenance and quality assurance should not be based on quality measurement, comparative assessment or quality control by an outsider (the government or inspectorate). Quality will be assured in the first place by internal quality care, i.e. constant and structural attention to quality by the institution itself and the units in the institution. It does not make sense to set up a system for external quality assessment without a good functioning system of internal quality care. Figure 2.1 shows the connection between internal quality care and external assessment.

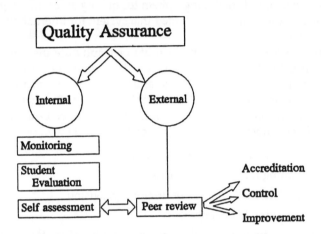

Figure 2.1. Internal and external elements of quality assurance

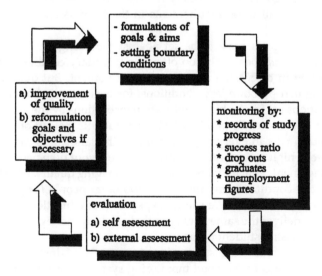

Figure 2.2. Internal quality assurance

Quality is the responsibility of all faculty members and students. In a way, quality is an individual matter. However, a curriculum is more than a number of classes. The quality of a curriculum is therefore a shared responsibility. For that reason, a faculty has to establish a good functioning system for quality assurance. Figure 2.2 shows the elements contained in a system for internal quality assurance.

The *goals and aims* of the institute or faculty are the frame of reference for the quality assurance. They must be formulated clearly and must meet scientific and societal requirements. The goals and aims should be clear about the concept of higher education, which a faculty holds. Of course this will often be a mixture of different concepts as distinguished by Barnett (1992):

- production of qualified manpower
- training for a research career
- efficient management of teaching provision
- extending life chances.

At the same time, the goals and aims should reflect the requirements set by the different stakeholders: students, academic world, employers, government, society at large. How does the faculty try to reconcile all those requirements in the formulated goals and aims?

But the goals have to be set against the background of the *boundary conditions*. Only too often the boundary conditions are forgotten in discussion about quality assessment. But quality is determined by boundary conditions, for example the boundary conditions set for the higher education institutions by the government. If you are allowed to select your students instead of being forced to take in everybody as in the Netherlands, it is easier to deliver a high success rate. If you can conduct your own personnel management, you are more capable of managing quality. Also the financial conditions are important. Too often people forget that quality has its price. We cannot expect higher education institutions to deliver the same quality with dwindling money resources and increasing student numbers.

A good *monitoring system* is necessary. Every institution or faculty must set up a good monitoring system. This contains for example the records of study progress, success ratios, dropouts, number of graduates, (un)employment figures. By using these instruments one can follow input, process and output. The faculty keeps its finger on the pulse and can take action whenever necessary.

Evaluation is the most important link in the process of quality assurance. Critical self-assessment must take place frequently, whether or not followed by peer review. The results of the evaluations and strengths/weaknesses analyses should lead to measures which can be taken in order to improve quality. The bottlenecks and weak points which are identified have to be eliminated.

Although quality control is no end in itself, as it should be integrated into general management policy, *management on the basis of quality* can be distinguished within the overall process of quality control. The results of the above activities may sometimes lead to management on the basis of quality. Whether it is a question of the maintenance of the qualitatively good, or of the strengthening of the qualitatively weak, measures have to be taken.

2.4 Self-Assessment, Cornerstone of EQA

Quality assessment has an internal and an external aspect: self-assessment and peer review, done by a review committee. The external quality assessment is never an end in itself, but rather an extension of the internal quality control. The hinge linking the external and the internal quality assessment is the self-assessment of the faculty, carried out prior to the visit by the review committee. A good self-assessment is as open and honest as possible. The self-assessment has a threefold purpose:

1. to stimulate internal quality management

2. to prepare internally for the visit by the review committee

3. to provide basic information for the review committee.

The results of the self-assessment should be laid down in a self-assessment or self-study report. This will be considered as confidential, although all staff members and students should be acquainted with the content. The layout and content of the self-study report should be related to the task of the review committee: to form an opinion about the programme in terms of content of education, educational process, organisation and management of the programme, and graduates. The self-study report should treat the following subjects (for a more detailed checklist see Chapter 3):

- **The place in the organisation.** Description of the specific organisational structure and the position of the faculty/discipline within the structure of the institution.

- **The students.** A description of the size and characteristics of the student intake. Success rates and dropout rates.

- **Brief description of the programmes.** Have objectives been formulated? To what extent do the objectives differ from those of similar programmes at other higher education institutions? To what extent are the objectives achieved?

- **The educational process.** What teaching methods are used? How are computers used in the courses? Are there specific problem areas? How are students assessed:

   a. in what way (multiple choice, open questions)
   b. when (sessional, finals)?

- **Programme organization and programme management.** How is the educational policy formulated? Is the policy of the faculty linked to the institutional policy? What is the policy in respect of the ratio of teaching to research? How large is the teaching load? How is attention given to internal quality management? Is there systematic evaluation? Which evaluation system is used? Is the study progress recorded? How does this work? Do these records lead to the early recognition of problems and to remedial and/or preventive actions aimed at the individual student or programme design?

- **The graduates.** Do prospective employers set standards which the graduate must meet? Can the future profession be clearly defined? Have these definitions changed over the years? Where do the graduates end up? What is the unemployment rate among graduates?

Appendices must be restricted to the most essential ones. In any event, the following appendices are to be included:

- list of academic staff with the following details: title, name, specialization, responsible for teaching in...

- list of the literature used in the core subjects in the main subject courses
- list of the important documents relating to the discipline (such as education reports, development plans, evaluation reports, educational policy plans, etc.) so that the review committee can, if it wishes, ask to see them.

In dealing with the subjects, a *description* is not enough; there must also be an *analysis* and the faculty/discipline's position on the question must be stated. This offers an opportunity to go more deeply into strong points and areas of concern. Finally, after the description of the existing situation and the analysis, the *intended means* of dealing with the shortcomings found must be indicated.

A self-assessment which has been performed well will be useful to the external committee. For faculties the question is, what information should they provide? This can result in strategic and defensive behaviour (Westerheijden 1990, Kallenberg and Krol-de Grauw 1992). Externally, the faculties may use the self-assessment reports as a public relations document instead of a critical analysis. Internally, the writer(s) of the report may use the text to express their own ideas about necessary changes without having the support of all faculty members.

Of course, a good self-evaluation initiates for a learning process, as we have seen for the Dutch universities (Vroeijenstijn 1991). Faculties reviewed in 1988, 1989 and 1990 had submitted about 80 self-study reports. Thirty reports have been scrutinized to see if the self-study reports fulfilled the expectations. To find out, the following questions were formulated:

- Is the self-study analytical and critical, so that the faculty can take actions based on the outcome? Or is it an expression of strategic behaviour and public relations document?
- What was the opinion of the review committee on the self-study?

The analysis of the self-studies showed that the quality of the reports differed strongly. The question whether the self-study is a useful instrument for internal quality enhancement and planning must be answered with all proper reserve. About 10 per cent of the reports contained a clear analysis as well as a description, and showed an attitude of self-assessment. The majority of the self-studies of 1989 created the impression that they were written only for the review committee rather than being used for critical self-reflection. In general the faculties did use the checklist of the VSNU, but this was at the same time the weakness. Although it is not always easy to draw a hard and fast line between description and analysis, we must conclude that the majority of the self-studies were very descriptive. Self-reflection was weak or sometimes lacking altogether. Not all self-studies had clearly formulated the problems the faculty had to deal with. The faculty had followed the checklist in the Guide and had tried to answer the questions for the review committee in a descriptive way. It seems that the majority of the faculties had not formulated the basic questions necessary for a good self-assessment:

- What are our goals, aims and objectives? Are they clearly stated? Are they useful? Why do we do what we are doing? Does consensus exist on the interpretation of the goals, aims and objectives?

- Is the programme designed with the realisation of the goals in view? Is the programme functioning well? Are there any problems? Do we control the input, the process and the output?

- Are the constraints for realisation of the goals satisfactory?

- Are the goals realised? How can we collect data systematically? What is the meaning of those performance indicators? (Kells 1988, Maassen 1989)

Of course faculties may adapt strategic behaviour and use the self-study as a public relations document, knowing that there will be a public report at the end of the external assessment. In the Dutch scene, however the review committees have only a few times made a remark to this effect. Although it is possible that a defensive attitude can account for the strong descriptive character, it seems more likely that it is caused by lack of experience with self-assessment in the way it is asked for.

Beside the internal role, the self-study plays a role as the most important source of information for the review committee. In general all the review committees stated that the self-studies provided very useful information. Only in a few cases did the review committee find a report very concise and not useful. A problem found in the majority of the self-studies is that of quantitative data.

All Dutch committees complained about it. So often, different definitions are used for calculation of the success ratio.

Our analysis of the self-studies of 1989/1990 leads to the conclusion that the majority of the reports gave worthwhile information to the review committees. They were a good starting point for the interviews and the formulation of questions by the committee. Although there was a beginning of self-reflection, it was too early to speak of real self-assessment. But realizing a good self-evaluation is also a process of learning by doing. Starting without a real tradition of self-assessment we may not expect too much. After all, Rome was not built in a day. Comparing the self-studies of 1989 and 1990 with the reports of 1991 and later, we see an improvement: the reports are becoming more and more analytical.

2.5 The Review Committee

The common features of most quality assessment models are self-assessment and assessment by peers, also called the committee of external experts or review committee. The traditional example of peer review is the referee system of scientific journals. An anonymous output of scientific activity (a manuscript) is judged by a few anonymous fellow scientists (peers) who are reputed to possess sufficient expertise on the questions addressed in the article. The norms and criteria they use in their judgements are the canons of the methods and the subject matter of 'good science' that are dominant in the particular discipline. In the context of quality assessment in higher education the concept of peer review is often used somewhat loosely (Goedegebuure *et al.* 1990). In the strict sense the peers are not always real peers, i.e. outstanding colleagues in the field, but often also people from industry, for example.

Regarding the review committee, there are a lot of questions. Who will choose the peers? Can we rely on the opinion of the peers? Are they not too subjective? Are they independent enough? Are they not too much involved? Is the country not too small to have a sufficient number of independent peers? In the opinion of Goedegebuure and his colleagues, 'the advantage of peer review lies in its high content validity. It is the only way to assess quality directly, without proxy indicators... The most important disadvantage of peer review is its subjectivity. The judgements always result from, in principle, unverifiable mental processes in the judges' (Goedegebuure *et al.* 1990).

Who are these peers, visiting the different faculties and giving their opinion about the quality of education? External quality assessment is done by outstanding experts in the field, but colleagues, nevertheless. It is very important that the discipline to be assessed has confidence in the committee. A faculty can hardly deny the judgements and recommendations of people who have been appointed as experts by the faculty itself. The faculty will accept the results and act on the recommendations more readily when they come from accepted peers rather than from experts 'parachuted in' from outside. Therefore the units should be involved, nominating experts for the committee. Of course, criteria can be given to be taken into account when selecting the members. For the more formal criteria, see Section 4.1. There are, next to the subject expertise, three prerequisites for a good committee. In the committee there should be enough understanding of the objectives of higher education, there must be an ability to put oneself in the shoes of the students and there should be enough familiarity with appropriate learning strategies in higher education. For the assessment of teaching/learning it is important that the foreign experts are competent in the language of the organising country. For the assessment of research the language may be English.

Given the fact of the faculties having influence on the nomination, will the external experts act as defenders of the discipline or will they try to act as objectively as possible? In the Netherlands the discipline is very much involved in nominating the members of the committee. Sometimes there is no problem, sometimes there is some bargaining (we do not like that person; if you agree with my candidate, I will agree with yours), but once appointed as a member, all experts try to be as objective as possible.

Often it is stressed that the experts should be independent. Apart from the fact that a totally independent expert does not exist, it may be necessary to have experts with no connections at all with the units to be assessed for a summative assessment, especially when decisions must be made about allocation of funds or closing down a department. In the case of formative assessment, when it is important to have people whom faculties are prepared to listen to, this is less important. Enough examples can be found of experts not defending their faculty or discipline, but critically evaluating them. Reading the reports of the Dutch committees, many remarks and comments can be found which support the policy of the minister rather than the policy of the faculty.

Although peer review is subjective, I do believe that a different committee visiting the same faculty would come forward with more or less the same findings and recommendations. This was for example the case with a Dutch peer review of electrical engineering (VSNU 1991a) and an international committee, visiting the same faculties (Vroeijenstijn, Waumans and Wijmans 1992).

In proposing experts, every effort must be made to cover the specializations within a discipline as fully as possible. This is particularly true if a number of (sub)disciplines (cognate curricula) are combined. The experts should be sought in the higher educa-tion institutions and among potential employers and, insofar as they exist, within professional organisations. In looking for experts from the higher education institutions it is wise not to choose just people who have retired or just experts who are still working in higher education institutions. A balanced distribution is desirable. The presence on the committee of someone with knowledge of educational processes is also important, because all experts have experience with teaching, but not always with curriculum design, psychology of learning, assessment design, etc. Furthermore it will be important to have at least one foreign expert (competent in the local language) on the committee to avoid 'provincialism' and to have an outsider's view in the committee. Too often people take things for granted as 'the national context' or 'regulated by law'. Someone from abroad may be able to refute the arguments.

A review committee has a dual function. On the one hand the purpose is to contribute to improvement; on the other hand the purpose is accountability. The function of improvement is strongly connected with the feedback which the committee may give to the faculty. The faculty may exchange views on educational problems in dialogue with 'peers'. The function of the committee is to comment upon the self-assessment. The review committee holds a mirror to the faculty. Because the committee also visits other faculties it has a good overview over possible solutions for prob-lems and can make suggestions for improvement. With regard to 'accountability' the committee of external experts can legitimate the internal quality assessment and management. The committee looks at what is done by the faculty with regard to quality management. Does a system for internal quality assessment exist? Does it work? The committee can prove to society (parliament, government, inspectorate) that the faculty takes serious care of quality and ensures quality. In the public report the committee gives an account of the state of the art of the education in the discipline concerned.

The task of the review committee is to form an opinion on the basis of information supplied by the faculty and by means of discussions held on the spot about the level of education and the quality of the educational process, including the organization of education and the quality of the graduates, and to make suggestions on quality improvement.

The committee is asked to form an opinion. In an improvement-oriented EQA system, the concept 'forming an opinion' should not be interpreted as 'sitting in judgement and handing down a verdict of good or bad'. Nor does it involve the approval of a programme or concern its accreditation or programme recognition, unless this task has been formulated beforehand.

The aim of external quality assessment is to detect, in a dialogue with the faculty, strong points and areas of concern. The committee's starting point is the objectives defined by the faculty. However, it will not always be possible to avoid the question whether the objectives formulated by this faculty are in line with the generally accepted objectives of a given programme or not.

A question which immediately arises is: on what criteria does a review committee assess education? Is it possible to formulate a set of criteria? The answer to this must be in the negative. It is not possible to design a series of criteria that apply equally to all disciplines. An expert knows implicitly what good education is or should be and what may be expected of a graduate. More explicitly, it should be possible to find the criteria in the objectives of the programme. A review committee must strive to make the implicit ideas on good education and good graduates more explicit. The committee will have to define for itself a frame of reference which it will use assessing the quality of the programme (see Section 4.2).

2.6 The Report of the Committee

The conflict between 'improvement' and 'accountability' arises particularly when the committee writes down its findings. Viewed in the light of 'improvement', it would be important to keep the report confidential. From several sides people stress that a public report endangers the function 'quality improvement' because faculties will adopt evasive behaviour (Kells 1988, 1989; Van Vught 1991). They are less willing for honest self-analysis and an open discussion with the peers. They are against exposing weaknesses, because they might be punished for that.

In the light of 'accountability', there will be pressure to publish as much as possible of the data, findings and conclusions. The outside world is interested in having as much information as possible about the faculty and the curriculum, and also about such matters as staff numbers, time spent on teaching and research and the cost per student.

The question of whether or not to have a public report is not difficult to answer, because the advantages of a public report are greater than the disadvantages:

- It is the only way to achieve the public function.
- By making the findings public, institutions learn about each other.
- It is good to have some pressure on faculties and higher education institutions by making a part of the findings public.

The expectations of the report highlight the different claims laid upon external quality assessment. The only way to reconcile the irreconcilable is by making beforehand an agreement between government and higher education institutions about the aspects to be treated in the report and about the way it will be presented. What does the government expect to find in the report? What kind of information? Given the agreement, government should not then put pressure on the system of external quality assessment by keeping watch to check if the committees keep to the deal.

When the higher education institutions do not have experience with a public report about their performance, it is possible that the approach may be different from the situation where there is already some experience, and that experience has shown that it does not result in direct interference from government.

We should make a distinction between the aspects that will be treated in the report and the way they will be treated. Because it is not possible to define 'quality of education', insight into quality can only be given by portraying certain aspects of quality:

- the programme: aims, characteristics of the programme and content
- the student and his/her education
- the graduates
- the academic staff
- internationalization
- internal quality assurance.

For more information see Table 4.7, page 105.

When a faculty is undergoing external quality assessment for the first time, the review committee will perhaps be advised to treat the topics in a more descriptive way without direct comparison with other faculties, because such a comparative approach may be felt threatening by the assessed faculties. However, experience in the Netherlands shows that, although the reports were not aiming at comparison, the outside world, especially the media, took the reports and made their own comparative overviews. Because lay-men had to translate the words of the experts, it was often done wrongly. That has been one of the reasons why the committees themselves chose a more comparative approach in the second cycle of EQA for the Dutch universities.

After the first approach of reporting only descriptively, there has been more and more interest in the comparative approach. The daily press write about the outcomes, and often in a comparative way. Students too are interested to see faculty X and faculty Y compared. But also faculties are interested to know their own position in the field: 'How do we perform compared with our colleagues?'

Although maybe not yet an attractive idea, the best way to encourage improvement and accountability is to treat the aspects mentioned above in a comparative way. An example regarding the goals and objectives is given in Table 4.7, page 105. By reporting in this way students get information about their education while simultaneously the outside world gets a picture of strengths and weaknesses of the programme. However, it must be clearly stated that a comparison of quality aspects does not mean ranking and is not aiming at it. Ranking is not appropriate, because adding the assessments of the individual aspects does not make sense; the detailed assessments will lose all their meaning.

2.7 The Follow-Up of the External Quality Assessment

The main effects of EQA are not only in the results (the final report of the review committee), but may be more important in the process itself: participating in an EQA process at faculty level changes the mentality. Apart from the results, a faculty which has been assessed will not continue to work exactly as before (in most cases). There is a kind of educational effect: people will be more conscious about quality and quality improvement, or even about the necessity to define objectives for the activity of the faculty.

Although external quality assessment already has a stimulating value, still an important question is what will be done with the outcomes? This will depend on the nature of recommendations. What type of outcomes may you expect from a review committee? Van der Weiden (1993) analysed twelve reports of Dutch review committees. Almost all committees had formulated minimum requirements for the programmes they were to evaluate and the committees checked to see if these minimum requirements had been. Fortunately most committees conclude that generally speaking the quality of the programmes is good. However, in some cases they are less satisfied. A few examples:

- In some cases there is no obligation for students to write an essay or to participate in research.
- Fairly often the committee members would give much lower marks for the essays than the teachers did.
- In some programmes students have too much freedom of choice so that there is a risk that they study elementary courses only or that their programme has no coherence.
- The reading assignments of some faculties are too 'local': teachers only teach their own views and do not pay enough attention to other views or approaches.
- The reading assignments of some faculties are too fragmentary: students do not read monographs, but only compilations of selected articles.

These remarks focused on the contents of the programmes. About the way of teaching the committees are much less specific. Some reports discuss the usefulness of lectures and emphasize that teaching in small groups would be more effective. They point out that not all teachers are able to deliver stimulating lectures. Other reports remark critically that first-year teaching is often left to young and inexperienced staff, while professors restrict themselves to the graduate students.

All reports dwell on the feasibility of the programmes. They all make a clear distinction between the theoretical possibility of completing the programme in four years, and the practical situation. Two committees concluded that the programme was not feasible in four years, not even when programme and students are of ideal quality. Five committees think that the workload is certainly not too heavy, and is even too light in the first year. This leads to complaints, also from the students, about the superficiality of the study programme. It has not enough to offer to the interested and gifted students. The fact that the workload is reasonable or even light does not mean that students of these programmes do graduate in four years. Committees think this is partly due to the students, who do not work hard enough, and partly to the organization of the programme (waiting periods, entrance requirements, examination regulations, etc.).

Five committees conclude that the programme is full and exacting, but that it should be possible to graduate in four years if the students are motivated and if the organization of the programme is improved.

It is clear from the reports that feasibility is not a matter of study hours and number of pages to be read. It is rather a matter of culture. Students do not work regularly enough. They adapt their study pace to the time-limits set by the law (six years) and by the grant system (five years).

We may conclude that review committees do not hesitate to describe in their reports weaknesses in the programmes, both regarding the contents and the feasibility. Because of the political impact of these issues there is no doubt that the higher education institutions and the faculties will use the observations and recommendations of the committees to further improvement of their study programmes as a follow-up of the assessment.

For the follow-up several conditions are important. The first is the acceptance of the review committee by the faculties. It is also important that after the visit there will be a dialogue in the faculty based on how to put the recommendations into practice. But the realization of recommendations is not always in the competence of the faculty. Therefore a dialogue between the faculty and the Executive Board of the institution is also necessary. The same applies, *mutatis mutandis*, to the dialogue between the institution and the Minister of Education and Sciences. Only when all people concerned take the recommendations of the review committee seriously will quality assessment and the work of the review committees be meaningful.

Those who wish to evaluate quality assessment using only the self-studies and the reports of the committees are making a mistake. The reports are important, but they are only the tip of the iceberg. The process of quality assessment is far and far more important. A lot is happening which will never be found in the reports.

It is known that faculties sometimes start with self-evaluation long before the formal announcement. There is already quality enhancement before the self-study report is written, but you will find no trace of it. The mere fact that a review committee is announced has a positive effect. The faculty wants to clean up the house before the committee arrives.

Just as the process of self-evaluation is more important than the self-study report, so also the actual visit is more important than the report of the review committee. When the faculty members meet the committee for the first time, they are a little tense. Often they still have the idea that the review committee comes as inspectors rather than as peers. But usually after the opening address of the chairman of the committee, the ice is broken. The faculty members like to discuss the educational problems with the members of the committee. They like the dialogue with the colleagues/experts. The discussion is very open. During the interview the review committee can make remarks and the faculty can draw conclusions based on the discussion. From the side of the faculty it is often said 'It was a hell of a job and the self-evaluation takes a lot of time, but it was all worthwhile.'

The publication of the report marks the end of the activities for the review committee. But the faculty cannot close the door behind the committee, lie back and relax. The faculty has to do something with the recommendations. It has to take action. It is not always easy to trace the effects of the review, but it is nevertheless agreed that the higher education institutions must render an account of what has been done or will be done with the results of the review in its development plans.

What role do self-assessment and external assessment play in self regulation? In the first place it is the faculty which has to make decisions about their 'mission' and the possibility of achieving it. The outcome of the self-assessment and the recommendations of the review committee should be discussed in the faculty. What to do for the improvement of the weak spots? What to do with the recommendations with regard to goals and aims? The programme? The process of teaching and learning? The educational management? Self-assessment and peer review help the faculty to steer its development.

But the faculty cannot do the job on its own. The HE institution too should have a good system of quality assurance and self-regulation. The executive board of the institution should open a dialogue with the faculty concerned, based on the results of the past quality assessment. At the moment we see in several higher education institutions the origin of a system for quality assessment at a central level (see, for example, Boetzelaer and Verveld 1990, Spaninks 1990, Ax 1990).

The faculties will work on the follow-up. But that is not enough. The discipline as a whole has to discuss the outcome of the review. It is one of the advantages of a nationwide or regional assessment that there will be a good overview of the state of the art of a discipline. The deans of the faculties concerned should meet regularly and discuss the results and the recommendations. This can be done in the framework of the assessment agency or the umbrella organisation. In the same way, the boards of the higher education institutions also should play a role in the discussion and in the follow-up. Decisions about the development of the higher education system, the natural expansion and contraction of the system, allocation of tasks, should be based on self-assessment and peer review.

2.8 Who Guards the Guardians?

When higher education institutions themselves are responsible for the external quality assessment, the question arises, 'Who assesses the assessors?' Being the owners of the system, it will become urgent to make clear to the outside world that it is not an old boys' network, protecting each other and stopping real shortcomings from becoming public. To that end it will be necessary to establish an authority outside the system in charge of the so-called meta-evaluation. In the Dutch case it is the Inspectorate, but it could also be a unit in the Ministry of Education and Science, or a body installed by the Minister.

As already stated, with the agreement of April 1986 on the main responsibility for EQA, the government and higher education institutions also agreed upon the role of the Inspectorate: 'The Inspectorate supervises the system of quality assessment and informs the Minister on its validity with respect to process and output. The task of the Inspectorate is called meta-evaluation' (Bresters and Kalkwijk 1990).

The Inspectorate describes meta-evaluation as 'the assessment of the carefulness with which the entire QA-system is set up by the institutions' (Kalkwijk 1991). The following criteria for meta-evaluation were given:

- EQA must cover all activities.
- It must be regular.
- External experts must be involved.
- Reports must be made public.

The Inspectorate itself added (Bresters and Kalkwijk 1990):

- The system must be transparent.
- There must be a follow-up.

The question is, 'What do we mean by meta-evaluation?' Meta-evaluation must take the aims of EQA as a starting point and the following questions should be asked:

- Are the goals and aims of EQA formulated clearly?
- Is the process to realise those aims controlled or, in other words, is the EQA done in the right way? How does the process happen?
- Do the products meet the formulated requirements?

Higher Education need not be afraid that there is no interest in what is going on as regards external quality assessment. Every year there is an exchange of views with the inspectorate, while civil servants at the Ministry of Education and Sciences also follow the process very critically. The media publish a lot about the outcomes of the assessments and ask questions. Every time that a report of a committee is published, the daily papers report on the findings. While the Inspectorate can be seen as the watchdog on behalf of the outside world, the Center for Higher Education Policy Studies (CSHOB) from the University of Twente can be seen as the scholarly conscience. Also, from within, critical sounds can be heard: from faculties and departments, from staff and students.

After five years, at the end of the first cycle of EQA of teaching/learning, the whole process has been evaluated. In that framework a lot of remarks have been made. As examples of comments and criticism, we will give the remarks made by the different parties concerned. It will be useful for the reader, because (s)he will be confronted with the same comments once started with EQA.

From the side of the assessed *faculties* the following remarks have been made (VSNU 1993a):

- The committees should pay more attention to the content of the programme and less to boundary conditions and structures.
- The aims of the EQA should be more clear; there is too much confusion regarding improvement and accountability.
- The committee should formulate more clearly its frame of reference; what are the criteria used by the committee?
- The committee should make more clear recommendations.
- The system should be less time-consuming.
- The time between visit and final publication should be shortened.
- The clustering of the programmes should be optimalised.

The *students* complained that (LSVB 1990, LSVB/ISO 1993):

- They were not informed about the coming visits of the committee.
- They were not always involved in the self-assessment.

- The committees should define clearly the concept of quality.
- There should be a student member on the review committee to ensure the students' interests.

From the side of the *experts* the following remarks were made (VSNU 1993a):

- The quality of the self-assessment should be improved; not all self-assessment satisfied the expectations.
- There is a need for better quantitative data.
- The presence of an educational specialist in the committee is very important.
- The introduction meeting should be longer.
- The programme of the visit is too tight.
- The clustering of the degree-programmes should be optimalized: more committees are needed.
- The meta-evaluation by the Inspectorate is often too bureaucratic and does not contribute to the improvement of the EQA-system.

From the side of the *government and the Inspectorate* for higher education the following comments regarding the system of EQA are made (Paardekoper and Spee 1990a,b; Spee 1990; Inspectie 1990b; Kalkwijk 1991):

- Quality should be defined plainly.
- Criteria and standards should be formulated clearly.
- Performance indicators should be more used in EQA.
- The reports of the committees are not uniform.
- The reports are not easily accessible to the public.
- So far, the committees have failed to formulate their frame of references.
- The committees dislike giving hard critical statements.
- The experts are not independent.
- Accountability must be improved and a better view on quality be given.

Looking at all these remarks, it will be clear that the system of EQA is not operating in darkness and obscurity; on the contrary, everybody is looking over the shoulder of the assessors.

2.9 Students and Quality Assessment

The contribution of students to the process of quality assessment is very important. On a programme level students should be involved in the evaluation of teaching, the staff and the programme. Student evaluations should have a permanent place in the internal quality assurance mechanism. The faculty should include the opinions of students in the self-assessment.

Students should also be involved in the self-assessment. At least one student should be a member of the self-assessment team. If the students feel that they have not been heard and if they not recognize themselves in the self-assessment, they should be able to hand a paper directly to the review committee.

During the site visits the review committee will also talk with student panels. Students should also have an opportunity to talk with the committee on an individual basis. Although many objections can be made to student opinions, they are a rich resource of information for a review committee. But of course those opinions need to be tested in the interviews with the staff.

Another way to involve students in the quality assessment is to nominate a student as a member of the review committee. In the Netherlands, since 1991 there have been some instances of this. An important role of a student member is to mobilize fellow students to express their views on the quality of the teaching/learning process.

Another important role for students is to follow critically what a faculty is doing with the recommendations of the review committee.

Chapter Three

Guidelines for the Self-Assessment

External quality assessment is not an end in itself, but rather an extension of the internal quality care. The hinge linking the external assessment and the internal quality assurance is the self-assessment which the faculty is required to present to the review committee. This self-assessment takes place in the period preceding the visit of the review committee.

In this chapter the importance of the self-assessment is considered further. Furthermore, guidelines are given and suggestions made concerning the implementation of the evaluation and the drawing up of the self-study. The manner in which the evaluation is carried out is determined by the faculty itself. There are, however, some rules which need to be adhered to with respect to the form and content of the self-study.

The checklist given in this chapter contains a series of topics to be discussed during the self-assessment. Regarding each topic one should keep in mind the following questions:

- What is the factual situation?
- What is your appraisal of the situation?
- How do you intend to cope with established shortcomings?

3.1 The Aims of the Self-Assessment

There are three aims for the self-assessment:

1. Stimulation of the internal quality control through analysis of strengths and weaknesses
2. Internal preparation for the visit of the review committee

3. Provision of basic information for the visit of the review committee.

The self-assessment which the faculty presents to the review committee determines to a very large extent the course and the effectiveness of the visit. The better the self-study, the better the committee will be able to carry out its work. Although the self-assessment report may be considered as a confidential document, it will be widely available in the faculty and sent to the review committee. Therefore, sometimes people tend to use the self-assessment report as a public relations document. An attempt is made to portray the situation in as flattering a light as possible. The committee then has to start its activities by breaking through the facade in order to arrive at the actual state of affairs. Another problem that will arise with some of the self-studies is that they remain at the level of description and are insufficiently analytical. An evaluation of one's own situation is missing.

A good self-assessment describes and analyses the situation as accurately as possible. The work of the committee members is then a matter of discussion of the self-evaluation, setting it against their own impressions concerning the quality of education rather than having to embark on a 'fact-finding' mission of their own.

3.2 The Approach to the Internal Evaluation

Ultimately it is the faculty which determines how the internal evaluation is carried out. However, it will be wise to make use of experiences gained on several occasions. On the basis of experience with self-assessment in Dutch universities, a number of suggestions may be made which can facilitate the process (given schematically in Table 3.1):

1. The self-assessment should never be the work of one single person.
2. Make a group responsible for the self-assessment.
3. This group should consist of some three to five people, under the chair of a coordinator appointed by the faculty.
4. A clear timetable should be set up, assuming a total amount of time available of some five or six months between the moment of the formal announcement and the actual visit.

5. The topics which are considered in the self-study (see below) should be distributed among the committee members and each member made responsible for the collection of information, the analysis and the evaluation of the situation.

6. The draft results should be discussed on as large a scale as possible. It is not necessary for there to be a consensus concerning the report; it is, however, necessary for as many people as possible to be aware of its contents.

7. Do involve students in the self-assessment as much as possible.

The objectives of the faculty or unit to be assessed form the starting point for the self-evaluation. In any adequately set up self-evaluation process the following questions will be addressed:

Table 3.1. The Organization of the Self-Assessment

Date	*Activity*
1 year before planned visit (= X)	Appointing the leader of the assessment process
	Composing the assessment team, including students
The following 6 months	Dividing the subjects
	Every person responsible for collecting information and data
	Writing a draft of the subjects
4 months after the start	Discussion of the drafts in the group
	Second draft
About 5 months after the start	Discussion of the second draft with all faculty staff and students during an open hearing
6 months after the start	Processing comments of the hearing in the final version
	Final version to the review committee

- What are the objectives? Are they clear, complete, appropriate and usable? Is there (internal) consensus concerning their interpretation?

- Are the educational programmes related appropriately to the objectives? Are programmes and services set up with the achievement of the objectives in mind? Does it appear that they work well? Do any problems arise with their implementation? How can any problems which arise be resolved?

- Are there adequate means available for the implementation of the programmes and services?

- To what extent are the objectives achieved? How can systematically collected data relating to the extent to which objectives are achieved be used? What is the significance of the data?

3.3 Conditions for the Self-Study Report

1. The self-study report is the reporting of the self-evaluation. That is to say, the self-study is not just descriptive, it is also analytical. It includes an evaluation of the problems. At the same time an indication is given as to how it is thought that problems identified will be dealt with.

2. The manner in which self-evaluations are carried out can vary; also the levels of who is to be involved in the discussion of the report will differ from one institution to another. Nevertheless, the responsibility for the self-study lies with the Faculty Board responsible for the programme(s) to be assessed.

3. Since it is the self-study which is of the most importance for the review committees, and these committees have to study a number of reports, it is important for all the reports to follow the same format. Directions concerning this are given below.

4. The self-study forms the starting point for the discussions between the review committee and the faculty. This implies that everyone who will be concerned in one way

or another with the discussions needs to be aware of the contents of the self-study.

5. The self-study should not extend to more than 30 or at a maximum 40 pages, excluding the appendices. Clear reference to any appendices taken up must be made in the main body of the report.

The quantitative data require special attention. The manner in which data will be presented is important, because the committees ask for comparability of information. So there is a clear need for the standardization of such data as student numbers, establishment of personnel, staff/student ratios, success rates, etc. In order to obtain uniformly presented data a number of tables have been given in these guidelines, but, of course, adaptations to the national context and national customs will be necessary.

In some cases cognate curricula will be involved in one single review. Since it is the self-study and self-assessment which form the basis of the quality assurance, the people responsible for each curriculum will have to carry out a self-assessment and a strengths/weaknesses analysis according to the checklist. Where more than one degree programme within a single faculty is involved, it is assumed that for each programme a self-assessment will be done. It is certainly advisable to establish with the faculty coordinator beforehand which topics should be dealt with at faculty level and which at the level of the programme. The faculty coordinator has the responsibility of ensuring that ultimately one single report is presented which includes the self-studies of the various degree programmes concerned, preceded by a general account from the faculty's perspective.

3.4 A Checklist for the Self-Study

Since there is a close connection between the work of the review committee and the self-assessment, the form and content of the self-study is closely associated with the task of the review committee. In order to reduce the activities to no more than is necessary it is urgently requested that an arrangement of topics as is given below should be followed, and all the aspects listed should be considered. In the checklist a number of 'points for attention' are given for each chapter which can be considered as topics to be addressed by the internal evaluation. If the checklist is followed carefully then it should be possible to arrive successfully in broad outline at a good strengths/weaknesses analysis. The checklist should not be seen as a list of questions to be answered and is not intended to be followed heedlessly; the list should rather be perceived as a manual to ensure that nothing is forgotten. If topics are listed which do not apply to the curriculum concerned, this may be indicated with a single comment. If there are topics which require particular emphasis in a certain degree programme, then that is also possible. Regarding each topic one should keep in mind the following questions:

- What is the factual situation?
- What is your appraisal of the situation?
- How do you intend to cope with established shortcomings?

The content of a self-study report is given in Figure 3.1.

Introduction
1. Goals, aims and objectives
2. The curriculum
3. Students' final essay, final research assignment and/or practical training
4. The student and his/her education
5. Facilities
6. The graduates
7. The staff
8. Internationalization
9. Internal quality assurance
10. Strengths and weaknesses
   Appendices

Figure 3.1. The content of a self-study report

Introduction

The self-study report starts with a description of the way the self-assessment has been carried out. Who was involved? Then a description of the organizational structure will be given. The discipline-oriented or subject-oriented approach of the external quality assessment does not always run parallel with the organizational position within the structure of the institution in which the unit to be visited finds itself; it is therefore advisable to commence the self-study with a chapter which indicates the structure and place taken up by the faculty/degree program within the organization. How is this structure perceived? Does it produce any obstacles tending to reduce quality, or does it work in such a way that the achievement of quality is facilitated?

Chapter 1: Goals, aims and objectives

**Table 3.2. Topics to be Discussed in Chapter 1:
Goals, Aims and Objectives**

Aims and objectives

What are the aims and objectives of the curriculum?

Are there requirements formulated by the labour market? How are these taken into account? Have there been changes in the professional profiles in recent years?

Are curriculum aims and objectives explicitly known to staff and students?

Are programme aims and objectives consistent with the institutional mission and aims?

To what extent are the objectives achieved?

Are there intentions to adapt the aims to changing contexts?

In what ways does this programme distinguish itself from other programmes at other institutions? What is the specific profile?

Translation of aims and objectives in the programme

How are the aims and objectives translated in the programme?

What is expected from the graduates with regard to knowledge, skills and attitudes?

How are those requirements processed in the programme?

Table 3.2 contains the aspects to be treated in this chapter. The main purpose of the chapter is to make clear the philosophy behind the programme: 'Why are we doing what we are doing?' Are the goals and aims clearly formulated and well known to staff and students? It is important to look at the connections of the faculty with labour market and professional bodies, as far as it is a curriculum concerned with a high professional profile, like engineering, medicine, law. What is the involvement of professional bodies in fixing the aims and goals?

Chapter 2: The curriculum

The aim of this chapter is to reflect on the curriculum and the coherency and to analyze the structure. It should be written in such a way that the review committee gets a clear picture of the programme. It will start with an outline of the programme according to the format in Appendix 4. Table 3.3 contains the aspects to be discussed and to be treated in this chapter.

Table 3.3. Topics to be Discussed in Chapter 2: The Curriculum

The programme

> Why did you choose this curriculum?
>
> Has the curriculum been changed radically in the past three years?
>
> What are the requirements for the coherency of the classes?
>
> Is the faculty content about the service-teaching delivered by other faculties?
>
> What is the ratio between the core curriculum and the optional courses?
>
> Are there bottlenecks in the programme?

Teaching methods

> What is the ratio between the different teaching methods (lectures, tutorials, practicals and self-study)?
>
> How far is the computer used in teaching/learning? The role of Computer Aided Instruction?
>
> Are there teaching methods that you do like to use but cannot because of the boundary conditions (e.g. number of students is to high for small group work).

Examinations

How are students assessed?

    a. In what ways (multiple choice, open questions)?

    b. When are they assessed (within or at the end of a course)?

Do the questions represent the final student objectives which have been laid down?

How are resits organized?

Who is responsible for the level of the exams?

Chapter 3: Students' final essay, final research assignment and/or practical training

At the end of many courses, a student has to write a major essay or carry out a final research assignment. In this part of the study a student can show his/her ability to integrate and manipulate the knowledge of various disciplines under the supervision of a mentor. For this reason it is important to make clear the role of the student work and assignment in the curriculum. In the appendix a list should be given of the titles of the last 25 final essays which students have submitted, and which were found to be satisfactory, with an indication of the grades awarded. Table 3.4 contains the aspects to be discussed in this chapter.

Table 3.4. Topics to be Discussed in Chapter 3: Students' Final Essay etc.

What is the weight of the major essay and/or research assignment in the curriculum (how many hours or how many credit points)

What are the criteria set for the major essay?

How and by whom is the major essay assessed?

Are there guidelines for the major essay/assignment?

How is the supervision regulated?

Is there a practical training required? Regulations?

Are there specific bottlenecks?

Chapter 4: The student and his/her education

In this chapter, information about the students should be given. In the first place some data should be given about student numbers and success rates. You need also to pay attention to student counselling, study planning, bottlenecks in the programme. Topics to be discussed are given in Table 3.5.

Table 3.5. Topics to be Discussed in Chapter 4: The Student and His/Her Education

What are the entrance requirements for the freshmen? Is there selection? How does it work?

Do the enrolment figures give rise to concern?

Is there a policy regarding enrolment figures? Activities to attract students?

Are there measures taken to enhance the quality of the influx?

Are the dropout rates acceptable?

Are you content with the success rates?

Are there fluctuations? If so, can they be explained?

Is it possible for an average student to finish the study in the programmed time?

Is student progress registered? How is that carried out?

Does the registration of progress lead to the timely signalling of problems?

How is the student in counselling organised? Does it function well?

Are students in trouble looked after satisfactorily?

Because of the need for comparability, the units to be assessed have to contain the same data (using the same definitions and the same sounding date). The following data are needed:

- number of freshmen (Table 3.6)
- total number of students (Table 3.7)
- success rates (Table 3.8).

After the quantitative data, it is necessary to pay attention to the study load. What are the programmed hours for lectures? Practical work? Self-study? Is the real time spent by the students in accordance with the programmed time? The data should be given in Table 3.9.

Table 3.6. Number of Freshmen

	Full-time			Part-time		
Year	Male	Female	Total	Male	Female	Total
1988/1989						
1989/1990						
1990/1991						
1991/1992						
1992/1993						
etc.						

Table 3.7. Total Number of Students

	Full-time			Part-time		
Year	Male	Female	Total	Male	Female	Total
1989/1990						
1990/1991						
1991/1992						
1992/1993						
etc.						

Table 3.8. Dropout and Completion Rates

Generation	Freshmen	Drop out after:		% graduates of the number of freshmen after			
		1 year	2 years	4 years	5 years	6 years	>6 years
1983/84							
1984/85							
1985/86							
1986/87							
1987/88							
1988/89							**
1989/90						**	**
1990/91					**	**	**
1991/92				**	**	**	**
1992/93				**	**	**	**
1993/94				**	**	**	**

Table 3.9. Total Study Burden of the Curriculum

Lectures	Practicals	Total contact hours	Major essay	Programmed self-study	Total programmed hours	Estimation of real spent hours

Chapter 5: Facilities

In this chapter a description will be given of all facilities: lecture halls, library, laboratory, etc. For the topics see Table 3.10.

Table 3.10. Topics to be Discussed in Chapter 5: Facilities

What is the situation concerning the facilities (lecture rooms, rooms for practicals, etc.)?

What is the situation concerning laboratories?

What is the situation concerning libraries?

What is the situation concerning computer equipment?

How large is the educational budget for the degree program?

What percentage of the budget is earmarked for material provision? What are the average costs per student?

Chapter 6: The graduates

It is important to reflect on the graduates. Do they really satisfy the expectations of the faculty? Do you know what they will do with the education? Is it easy to find a job or are there many unemployed? For topics see Table 3.11.

Table 3.11. Topics to be Discussed in Chapter 6: The Graduates

Is it known where graduates find employment?

What is the situation concerning graduate unemployment?

Are there any contacts with alumni?

What is the opinion of alumni with respect to the educational programme?

Chapter 7: The staff

Quality depends very much on the quality of the staff. Therefore you have to reflect on this: is the size of staff large enough to cover all subjects? Are the qualifications of the staff adequate. See Table 3.12.

Table 3.12. Topics to be Discussed in Chapter 7: The Staff

What is the number of personnel (see Table 3.13)? Are there any problems regarding staffing? Age distribution? Are any vacancies difficult to fill?

What is the student/staff ratio? Graduate/staff ratio? (see Table 3.14.)

What policy is followed with respect to the allotment of academic staff to teaching and research? Is a conscious choice made of lecturers for the basic programme?

How much time is spent on service teaching for other faculties?

Is there any policy with respect to the allotment of lecturers to informal lectures, to supervision of essays/master theses, practicals and work experience?

What role do didactic qualifications play in the furtherance of one's academic career?

Are there staff development programmes?

Table 3.13. Staffing (Academic and Non-Academic Staff): Number of Persons and Full-Time Equivalents

Number of persons (x) and Full-time equivalents (y)						
Year	Full pro-fessors	Associate professors	Assistant professors	Research assistant	Others	Total academic staff	Non-academic staff
1992	x (y)						
1993							
1994							

Chapter 8: Internationalization

Looking at the developments in Europe and the importance of student exchanges, attention needs to be paid to the activities in the field of 'internationalization' of education. What is the participation of the faculty in the ERASMUS programme or in other programmes for student exchange? Has the faculty special interest in international contacts? With which institutions do you have contacts?

Table 3.14. Student/Staff Ratio and Graduate/Staff Ratio

	Fte-teaching acad.staff	Number of students	Number of graduates	Number of students per staff member	Number of graduates per staff member
1992					
1993					
1994					

Chapter 9: Internal quality assurance

This part of the analysis is the most important one, because quality has to be maintained continuously. The topics given in Table 3.15 need to be discussed. It is also important to stress the role of students and staff in the evaluation. Is there a regular student appraisal of staff and a regular staff appraisal of management?

**Table 3.15. Topics to be Discussed in
Chapter 9: Internal Quality Assurance**

Does a systematic record for student progress exist?

Does a record for initial employment of graduates exist?

Does a systematic record for staff research and development grants exist?

Does a systematic record for staff publications exist?

Is there systematic evaluation? If so, in what way is it done? How are students involved in the evaluation of education? What is done with the results? Is any feedback given to the students?

Who is responsible for innovation of the curriculum? How is it done?

Chapter 10: Strengths and weaknesses

In the last chapter you will be requested to summarize the strong points and the weak points in the unit under assessment. What are you planning to do for enhancement?

Appendices

The appendices need to be restricted in number to those which are strictly necessary. Should any appendices be included, then their relevance must be made clear where appropriate in the main body of the text. In any case, however, the following appendices need to be included:

- a list of the names of the academic staff with the following data: title, name, specialization, responsible for education in...

- a list of the literature drawn upon in the core curriculum

- a list of the last 25 major essays submitted and found to be satisfactory, together with the grades awarded

- a list of the most important papers concerning the programme (such as development plans, evaluation reports, educational policy plans, etc.) so that the review committee may peruse these should they wish to do so.

3.5 Concluding Remarks

After finishing the self-assessment and after discussion of the report with staff and students, the faculty sends 10 copies of the report to the assessment agency. The agency will forward the report to the review committee.

Make enough copies for staff and students, because one of the first questions the committee will ask during the visit is, 'Are you acquainted with the self-assessment and do you recognize yourself in the report?'

Chapter Four

Guidelines for the Review Committee

The review committee is the pinning-link between the improvement-orientation and the public function of EQA. The role of the review committee is not an easy one. It has to combine different functions. The committee will:

- check the outcomes of the self-assessment
- reflect on the self-assessment
- have a dialogue and discussion with staff and students
- act as accountant.

The committee is trying to combine two missions. The review committee should listen to the faculty and act as colleagues, using their expertise and experience to offer advice and recommendations. At the same time the committee has to write the public report, in which the outside world will be notified about the quality or aspects of quality of the faculties. It will not always be easy to combine the divergent roles.

This chapter contains guidelines for a review committee. These guidelines are based on experience in the Dutch situation, as was the case with the guidelines for the self-assessment in Chapter 3. Of course, one has to adapt the advice and recommendations to the national context.

The following topics will be treated:

- the composition of the review committee
- the preparation for the review
- what is the committee looking for?
- the site visit
- the formulation of the findings, using a checklist
- the report of the committee.

4.1 The Review Committee

A review committee has 5 to 7 members. Membership of a review committee should include:

- a chairperson, not working in one of the faculties to be visited. He or she does not need to be an expert in the field, but should have the confidence of those who are. If possible the chairperson should have experience with management structures in higher education institutions and the developments that have taken place in the last few years
- two experts in the field of the subject area
- an expert in the field from the employment area taking up graduates and/or from the professional association
- an expert from abroad (but because the visit will be done in the vernacular, this member must master the language)
- an expert in the field of education/learning processes. An expert from the area of research and development of higher education may be considered, or an expert in the teaching of the subject.

The secretariat of the committee is taken care of by the body organizing the review.

There is often a tendency only to nominate retired people on the grounds that they are more independent (and have more time available). However, it is also important to have members still working in the field and having knowledge of recent developments.

The terms of reference

In general, the task of a committee can be described as:

- To form an opinion on the basis of information supplied by the faculty and by means of discussions held on the spot about the standard of education and the quality of the educational process, including the organisation of education and the standard of the graduates; in assessing quality, the committee must look at the requirements/expectations of the student, the faculty/discipline and society, and prospective employers in particular.

- To make suggestions on quality improvement.

Operationalization of the terms of reference

A committee trying to fulfil its task will meet a lot of problems. Because of its general formulation, the committee will tend to form opinions about everything. Therefore, for the benefit of the committee and the faculty, the terms of reference have been operationalized into a number of questions (see Table 4.1). These questions are connected with the aspects the committee will report on. The committee has as task to answer the questions based on the information in the self-assessment and on information obtained during the interviews. When the committee has succeeded in answering the questions, then it has completed its job.

Table 4.1. Questions to be Answered by the Committee

---

1 Aims and objectives

1.1 The aims

1. Are the aims and objectives clearly stated?
2. Are the aims and objectives a good mixture of scientific orientation and practice orientation?
3. Are the formulated aims and objectives realistic and achievable, looking at the boundary conditions like the nominal duration of study and the starting level of the students?
4. Do aims and objectives represent the minimal requirements as formulated by the committee?
5. Are staff and students acquainted with the aims and objectives?

1.2 Translation of the aims and objectives in the programme

1. Does the programme offer enough possibilities to develop a capability for problem-solving?
2. Does the programme offer enough possibilities to develop an understanding of the relation between the programme and professional duties in the future job?

3. Does the programme offer enough possibilities to develop an ability to maintain professional competency through lifelong learning?
4. Does the programme further independent and critical thinking?
5. Does the programme further independent learning and work?
6. Is the programme coherent?
7. Is the programme up-to-date?

2 *The curriculum*

2.1 *The structure and content of the programme*

1. Are the aims and objectives translated in the programme in an adequate way?
2. Does the programme contain the necessary basic courses?
3. Is the level of the basic courses satisfactory?
4. Is the supply of optional subjects satisfactory?
5. Can the programme in general be assessed as being at academic level?

2.2 *Teaching methods*

1. Is the ratio between the different teaching methods (lectures, tutorials, practicals and self-study) optimum?
2. Are the possibilities to use the computer in education utilized satisfactorily?

2.3 *Examinations*

1. Do the preliminary examinations and final examinations reflect the content of the curriculum?
2. Is the level of examinations satisfactory?
3. Are the frequency and the sequence of the preliminary examinations correct?
4. Are the exam procedures correct?

2.4 *Student skills*

1. Is the attention to written communication satisfactory?
2. Is the attention to oral communication satisfactory?
3. Are the experiences of the students in using the computer satisfactory?
4. Are the laboratory experiences of the students satisfactory?

3 Students' final essay, final research assignment and/or practical training

1. Is the level of the final essay (if any) satisfactory?
2. Is the supervision of the final work adequate?
3. Do the requirements with regard to the final work reflect the weight of this part of the study?
4. When there is practical training, are the regulations satisfactory?

4 The student and his/her education

1. Is the preliminary education of the freshman adequate?
2. Is the selection of students adequate?
3. Is the dropout rate in the first year acceptable?
4. Is the overall pass rate satisfactory?
5. What is the opinion of the committee about the average duration of the study?
6. Does the programmed study load fit in with the real study load?
7. Can the majority of students finish the study in the programmed time?
8. Does the programmed study load fit in with the real study load?

5 Facilities

1. Are the student teaching and laboratory areas adequate?
2. Is the equipment used essentially for teaching purposes on the whole adequate?
3. Are the library resource materials available to staff and students adequate?
4. Are the computer facilities available to staff and students adequate?
5. Do the laboratory facilities reflect the requirements of the programme satisfactorily?
6. Are the facilities available to staff and students accessible after hours?

6 The graduates

1. Does the graduate deserve the Master's degree?
2. Is the graduate satisfactorily equipped for the labour market?
3. Can graduates very easily get a job?

7 The staff

1. Is the competency/qualifications of the academic staff satisfactory?
2. Is the level of scholarship as shown by scientific and professional publications satisfactory?
3. Is the size of the academic staff large enough to cover all of the curricular areas?
4. Is the balance between research and teaching responsibilities of academic staff satisfactory?
5. Are staff development programmes satisfactory?
6. Is the student/staff rate satisfactory?
7. Is the number of professors in the basic courses satisfactory?
8. Is the attention education and research well-balanced?

8 Internationalization

1. Does the faculty participate in ERASMUS and other European exchange schemes?
2. How Involved is the faculty with internationalization?

9 Internal quality assurance

9.1 The self-assessment

1. Was the self-assessment critical and analytical?
2. Was the self-assessment useful for the committee?

9.2 Internal quality assurance

1. Does the faculty maintain a formal and systematic record of student progress?
2. Does the faculty maintain a formal and systematic record of initial employment of graduates?
3. Does the faculty maintain a formal and systematic record of staff research and development grants?
4. Does the faculty maintain a formal and systematic record of staff publications?
5. Does the faculty have a good evaluation system, including student evaluation?
6. Does there exist a good climate for regular quality assurance?

Looking at a national context it may be necessary to add some other questions and bring them to the attention to the committee. The formulated questions will be added to the checklist for the committee and become aspects to be treated in the report.

4.2 The Preparation of the Site Visits

Study of the self-assessment reports

As soon as the faculty has sent the self-assessment report to the assessment agency, it will be sent to the members of the committee. It is very important that every committee member study this report carefully before the committee comes together in the preliminary meeting. As a starting point for the discussions during the preliminary meeting, every member is invited to answer the questions with regard to the self-assessment reports as formulated in Table 4.2.

Table 4.2. Questions to be Answered Regarding the Self-Assessment Report

Is the report sufficiently critical and analytical?

Are the problems, facing the faculty clearly formulated?

Has the faculty indicated clearly how it will cope with the problems?

Are you able to form a picture of the content of the curriculum, given the description in the report?

Are the aims satisfactorily operationalized?

Are the aims and goals, in your opinion, satisfactorily translated into the programme?

May the curriculum be assessed as an academic curriculum in your opinion?

Is the curriculum well-balanced?

Can the programme, as described in the report, be done in the programmed time?

Is it in your opinion possible to deliver good graduates with this curriculum?

By answering these questions, the member is not tied to a final judgement. It is only a first impression, based on written information. During the site visits there will be time for a more well-informed opinion. The committee member is requested to send his/her comments on the self-evaluation to the secretary of the committee three weeks before the plenary meeting. The secretary will summarize the comments of all committee members.

Assessing student work

At the end of many courses, a student often has to write a final essay, also called a final thesis or major essay. In this part of the study a student can show his/her ability to integrate and manipulate the knowledge of various disciplines under the supervision of a mentor. For this reason it is important that the committee also studies examples of this final work. The best way to do this is to

Table 4.3. Aspects to be Treated when Assessing Final Essays

Are the aims of the essay and/or the hypothesis satisfactory formulated?

Does the author stick to the formulated aims?

Is the argumentation logical and consistent?

Are the conclusions consistent with the presented material?

Is the method used the right one?

Does the author present his/her material in such a way that the research can be checked?

Are the basic concepts clearly defined and operationalized?

Are the chosen method and technique applied correctly?

Are notes and references clearly and consistently edited?

How is the style of writing to be assessed?

How is the composition of the essay?

Is the author well acquainted with the literature in the field of his/her subject?

When you mark the essay with a mark on the scale 1 to 10 (10 = very good), what mark will you give?

---

ask the faculties to send a list with titles of final essays which have passed the assessment. The secretary sends the list to the member, who may mark the essays he or she wishes to read. Every member reads at least two essays per faculty to be assessed. In assessing the essays, the member will give his/her opinion about the aspects mentioned in Table 4.3.

Every member will return the judgement at the latest a fortnight before the plenary meeting. The secretary will summarize the opinions per faculty.

The formulation of the frame of reference

Every expert has implicit ideas about the quality of a curriculum or the qualities of the graduates. However, individual frames of reference will differ, due to different backgrounds and different experiences. Therefore, one of the first tasks of a review committee is to make the implicit opinions explicit and to formulate a frame of reference acceptable to all committee members. Against this background, the committee will assess the faculties.

The frame of reference is not a sketch of an ideal curriculum, but should be considered as a set of minimum requirements for a programme as seen by the committee. It contains the minimum requirements for a graduate in a special field. What makes a biologist a biologist? An electrical engineer an electrical engineer?

The chairman and the secretary formulate a first draft of the frame of reference that will be discussed during the first meeting. Table 4.4 gives some aspects which should be taken into account when formulating the frame of reference.

Table 4.4. Formulating a Frame of Reference

What, in the opinion of the committee, are the aims and objectives of the curriculum?

What are the minimum requirements for such a programme, with regard to the academic level and looking at the requirements set by society?

What are the minimum requirements regarding knowledge, skills and attitudes of a graduate?

What are the special requirements set by the labour market?

Using the frame of reference, a committee always should keep in mind that the aims and objectives as formulated by the faculty have to be the starting point for the assessment by the committee. It is not the intention to impose criteria and standards from outside, for example, a professional body. However, the aims and objectives formulated by the faculty can be discussed as regards their being of academic level, complete and clear.

If the external assessment has as aim the accreditation of the programme, the frame of reference will be provided by an outside body, for example the government or a professional body.

4.3 The First Meeting of the Committee

Roughly two months after receiving the self-assessment reports, a two-day meeting will be organised for the committee. The purposes are:

1. further explanation of the working method of the committee. What is expected from the committee?
2. agreement on the frame of references
3. discussion of the self-assessment reports.

Further explanation of the working method

As already stressed, it is important that a committee uses the same working method for all faculties to be assessed. There is a risk that a committee will discuss some topics in one faculty and others in another faculty. Equal treatment is required: that is the reason for standardization of the procedures. As far as there are still obscurities, they will be explained now.

Agreement on the frame of reference

The secretary has sent the draft of the frame of reference to the committee. The first part of the meeting will be used for discussing the draft and for agreeing on the final version.

Discussion of the self-assessment reports

The secretary will make a first sketch of each faculty. (S)he will make use of the format for the faculty report (see Appendix 2). In this outline quantitative data and some important facts will already be given. Also the answers of the members to the questions regarding each report (see Table 4.2) will be summarized by the secretary. The judgement of the essays will be added too. Those 'faculty sketch' and the self-assessment reports are the bases for the discussion. The discussion will end in:

1. agreement on the assessment of the self-evaluation
2. formulation of specific questions to be asked during the site visit
3. decision as to whether additional information is wanted.

The committee as a team

The two-day meeting is also important for making the committee into a team. Many a review committee has complained that the committee did not act as a team until after the first site visit. Through the two-day meeting, the intensive discussion on the frame of reference and the reports, the committee will become a unit and will start the site visits as a team.

4.4 What is the Review Committee Looking For?

During the first meeting some topics will be brought up in discussion. What is quality? Is it possible to formulate criteria and standards? What is the role of performance indicators? Should a committee attend lectures? What is the connection with research? The questions of quality, criteria and standards, the role of PIs and the connection between education and research have already been treated in Chapter 1. We will now address the question, 'What is the committee looking for?'

There are four main questions when assessing the quality of education:

1. Are the goals and aims clearly formulated
2. How are these translated in the curriculum?
3. Do the exams reflect the content of the programme and courses?
4. Does a graduate really have the expected knowledge, skills and attitudes?

In Figure 4.1 the factors defining the quality are given.

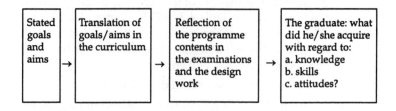

Figure 4.1. Factors defining the quality

As already said in Chapter 1, quality is a multi-interpretable concept. We cannot speak about *the* quality, we have to speak about qualities or aspects of quality. The different factors which influence the quality of the educational programme can be represented as a series of concentric layers (see Figure 4.2).

The ultimate quality of an educational programme is determined by a number of factors. In the first place it is strongly dependent on the quality of the lecturers and the manner in which knowledge is transferred. This is difficult to judge at first hand without spending a great deal of time in lectures and seminars. Indirectly, an opinion can be formed by drawing on the comments of students with respect to the educational provision, the extent to which the lecturers are able to receive didactic training, and the extent to which didactic qualities are taken into account in the appointment and promotion of staff.

The quality of the educational programme is further determined by the content and the level of the subject matter taught. The content is again strongly dependent on the objectives, and the manner in which these are translated into final student assignments. To a certain extent the course description gives some insight into the course content.

Questions which can be asked concerning this are related to the consistency of the programme, the underlying philosophy (why has this programme in fact been chosen?). Are the programme elements necessary for practice in the professional field included? Does the programme conform with recent developments in the discipline? Is the educational programme of a sufficiently high scholastic level? Does the content of the educational programme satisfy the requirements of occupation and profession? In order to

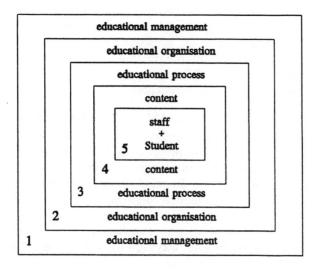

Figure 4.2. Components of the quality of teaching/learning

form an overall view of the educational level of the programme the committee members will have to continue to collect and place together the separate pieces of a jigsaw puzzle. The necessary knowledge can be accumulated from the study of the following:

- the lists of the used literature
- final project work
- tests and examination questions
- course descriptions and readers.

The experts in the committee are expressly chosen so that, on the basis of the available information, they will be able to form a picture of the content and level of the educational programme in a very short time.

THE EDUCATIONAL PROCESS

Other than through the direct transfer of knowledge, content and level, the quality of the educational programme is also determined by the educational process. Apart from considering an individual teacher, it can be seen whether in general the most appropriate instructional methods are used for transfer of knowledge to the students. Has the programme been so set up that it can be completed by a student in the prescribed time without too many difficulties? How has the programme been built up? Are there unnecessary bottlenecks? Does the programme match up with the reasonable expectations of students?

EDUCATIONAL ORGANIZATION AND EDUCATIONAL MANAGEMENT

The given restraints and educational policy also determine the quality of the educational programme. What are the conditions under which the degree programme must give shape to the educational process? What is the relationship between teaching and research? What is the situation concerning the study load? What policy is followed with respect to education? An important aspect of educational organization and management is the structural quality assurance. In what ways are these attended to? What is done as a result of evaluation?

An important question is, 'Should a committee attend lectures?'

The quality of education depends foremost on the interaction between staff and student. It is logical that the committee should attend lectures, tutorials and working groups. However, given the short time for the site visit it is quite impossible to do so. To get an impression of how things are going in the lecture halls, a committee can agree to walk into a lecture hall 'in action' and feel the climate. However, it must be stressed that it is not a task of the committee to assess an individual staff member.

4.5 The Programme of the Site Visit

The secretary designs a programme for the site visit in consultation with the faculty according to a given format (see Table 4.5). Beforehand, appointments are made with whichever staff members and students the committee would like to talk with.

The interviews start with a discussion with the *writers of the self-assessment report*. In this interview the committee can ask for clarification of some obscurities and explanation of some topics that are not totally clear.

The *interviews with the students* are purposely planned to take place before the interviews with the staff members. The students are a very rich source of information, but the information needs to be checked and tested against the ideas of the staff members. The interviews with the students are important in order to get insight into the study load, the didactic qualifications of the staff, the coherency of the programme, to find if they are acquainted with the goals and aims, the organisation of the curricula and the facilities. The interviews with the students should be held in the absence of staff members, so they can speak freely. The size of the groups of students is ideally about ten each time. The best is to talk with about 10 students in the first year, 10 students in, say second and third year and 10 students nearly at the end of their study. The composition of the student panels require special attention. It is important that the group is as far as possible representative of the whole student population in that field; not only the good ones but also the less gifted students. It is better not to leave the invitation of students to the faculty or the staff. The best way is to ask a student organisation (if there is any) to nominate the students. If there is no such organisation, the secretary of the review committee will invite students at random.

The *interviews with the staff members* will be used for a discussion on the content of the curriculum, the aims and objectives ('Why did you choose this programme as you have?'). Other topics to be discussed are the examinations, the final essay (if there is any), the final research projects, etc. It is advisable to talk with groups of about 10 staff members and with the plenary committee. Make subcommittees only when it is absolutely necessary.

Table 4.5. Draft Programme for a Site Visit

16.00 hours on the day preceding the proper visit, the committee members find each other in the hotel. There is a meeting for:
- discussion on the draft report of a preceding visit
- discussion of the topics requiring special attention during this visit

17.00–18.00 reception of the authorities of the university and/or faculty

18.00 dinner for the committee.

Day 1

09.00–17.00 interviews with:

- the writers of the self assessment report
- students
- staff members
- curriculum committee/examination committee
- student counsellors

18.00–19.00 dinner for the committee

20.00 short meeting for discussion on the findings of the day and fixing the programme for the next day.

Day 2

09.00–10.00 interview with faculty board

10.00–11.00 open hour/time for additional interviews

11.00–12.30 visit to lecture halls, practical rooms, library, laboratories

14.00–16.30 formulation of the findings

16.30–17.00 oral presentation of the findings to faculty board

---

Other interviews will be with *members of a curriculum committee* and with *members of the committee responsible for the examinations*. This will depend on the national context. During the interview with the curriculum committee the way the curriculum is kept up to date will be discussed and how innovations are planned and realized, etc. The interview with the examination committee must make clear how the quality of the examinations and degrees is assured.

A part of the programme is intended for a look at the facilities: lecture halls, working group rooms, laboratories, practical rooms, libraries, etc. During this tour, it will be possible to feel the climate in a lecture hall with students. For visiting the facilities, the committee can be split up into small groups.

It will be wise to organize an *open hour* where individual staff members and individual students can talk with the committee. The secretary should ensure that this open hour is well publicized within the faculty. A staff member or student who wishes to talk with the committee goes directly to the secretary. The faculty does not need to know who is talking with the committee.

The formulation of the findings

The last afternoon is intended for the formulation of the findings. There are about two-and-a-half hours available for this difficult task. The best method is as follows:

1. Completion of the checklist by the individual members
2. Discussion of topics to be treated in the oral report
3. Formulation of the oral report by chairman and secretary.

THE CHECKLIST

The first hour will be used by the members to complete the checklist (see Appendix 3). It is very important to fill up the list on the spot. Do not take the list home for completion. Of course a mature judgment is important, but so is a first impression. Another reason for doing it at the end of the visit is that the secretary needs the list in order to prepare the draft report on this faculty.

The committee members are requested to give a mark between 1 and 10 for different aspects. The reason for this is twofold: on the one hand it confronts, after processing of the data by the secretary, the committee with possible discrepancies between the verbal judgements and the judgements with marks. ('We are all saying that a certain aspect may be assessed as good; however, looking at the figures we are only awarding it 'adequate'. How is that possible?') On the other hand this marking is necessary for the final report.

To have some idea of the value of the figures, you can keep the following ideas in mind:

- Give 1–3 when in your opinion this aspect should be considered as critical. The university board or faculty board have to act directly. Something has to be done and people cannot wait.

- Give 4–5 when in your opinion this aspect is unsatisfactory. It must be improved, but it is not directly threatening the quality of the graduate.

- Give 6–7 when in your opinion the situation is satisfactory. The faculty may be satisfied, but there is no reason to be proud.
- Give 7–8 when in your opinion this topic can be assessed as more than satisfactory, but not excellent.
- Give over 8 when in your opinion this topic can be assessed as excellent. The faculty can be proud of it and it is certainly a strong point.

In the final report the marks will be translated into the following symbols:

a score of less than 4	– – = critical
a score of 4–5	– = unsatisfactory
a score of 6	□ = satisfactory
a score of 7–8	+ + = good
a score of more than 8	⊕ = excellent

DISCUSSION ON TOPICS FOR THE ORAL PRESENTATION

After completing the checklist, the chairman will make an inventory of the topics to be treated in the oral presentation. Therefore, it will be handy to mark the topics in the checklist. Distinction can be made between: main items of the findings; and critical comments regarding topics, not to be included in the public report, but rather to be brought forward in the oral presentation because it concerns only the faculty and has no value for the public. Based on experience it seems that about 45 minutes is needed to discuss the topics.

FORMULATION OF THE ORAL PRESENTATION

Chairman and secretary will formulate the content of the oral presentation, based on the discussion with all members. In this 45 minutes, the other members can use the time for visiting facilities, if this is still needed.

The oral presentation

The oral presentation at the end holds a special position in the process. There are sometimes findings and conclusions not really suitable for the public report but which the committee would like to make a critical statement about. In that case, the oral presentation can be used to formulate strongly worded recommendations. In order to do justice to this principle, the oral presentation is not public: the committee reports to the faculty board.

The chairman should stress that this is an interim report: some conclusions may change during the 'tour' of the committee. It is advisable not only to mention the weaknesses, but also the strengths of the faculty.

4.6 The Report

The faculty report

After a visit to a faculty, the secretary writes a first draft of the faculty report, using the completed checklists and the minutes of the oral presentation. The secretary will use the format for the faculty report (see Appendix 2).

The draft will be discussed at the beginning of the next visit. The second draft will be sent to the faculty for comments. The committee decides what to do with the comments.

The final report

For the final report see the format in Appendix 4. In the final report a distinction will be made between a general part and a specific part, addressed to the faculty. Both parts will be written according to a fixed format. There are several reasons to do so:

- It is desirable to assess all programmes in the same way.

- Although it is not meaningful to compare the reports of the different committees, it is necessary that 'giving a good view of the quality' will be done in the same way for all disciplines.

In the general part of the report the topics to be treated are given in Table 4.6. The topics will not only be treated in a descriptive way, but also in a comparative way. An example is given in Table 4.7 concerning the opinion of the committee regarding the formulation of aims and objectives.

Table 4.6. Topics to be Treated in the Report

1. The programme: aims, characteristics of the programme and content	*4. The academic staff*
the aims & objectives	staffing
programme characteristics	qualifications of the staff
contents of the programme	student/staff ratio and graduate/staff ratio
level of examinations and methods for assessment	staff management
students' skills	
level of final essay and final projects	
2. The student and his/her education	*5. Internationalization*
student numbers: freshmen + total numbers	participation in ERASMUS etc.
dropouts and completion rates	international contacts
average duration of study	
study burden	
organisation of the programme	
study counselling	
facilities/infrastructure	
3. The graduates	*6. Internal Quality Assurance*
the level of the graduate	the self assessment
labour market perspectives	what is done with the outcomes of preceding assessment, if there has been one?
	the way of evaluation
	connections with alumni

Table 4.7. Example of a Comparative Table
in the Report of a Committee

Aims and objectives	A^1	B	C	D	E	F
Are the aims and objectives are clearly stated?	□	□	□	+ +	+ +	+ +
Are the aims and objectives realistic and achievable, looking at the boundary conditions?	–	–	□	+ +	+ +	+ +
Are the aims and goals of an academic level?	□	□	□	+ +	+ +	+ +
Do the goals and aims represent the minimum requirements?	□	□	□	+ +	+ +	+ +

– – = critical; – = unsatisfactory; □ = satisfactory; + + = good;
⊕ = excellent
1 A to F stand for the assessed faculties

Although people may shrink from comparisons, several reasons can be given for them:

- A faculty not only likes to know the judgement about its own quality, but also likes to know its position in this field.
- Such comparisons may also be useful to get more idea about the international position in this field.
- Quality assessment not only has an improvement orientation, but also a public function: to give the outside world insight into quality.
- If the committee does not give these comparative tables, the outside world (the media) will make them, translating the words of the committee into symbols. Because they never participate in a visit, it often will be wrong and damaging.
- The committee is confronted with discrepancies between written judgements and the assessment by means of symbols.

However, it must be clearly stated that a comparison of quality aspects does not mean ranking and is not aiming at it. Ranking is not appropriate, because adding the assessments of the individual aspects does not make sense; the detailed assessments will lose all their meaning.

Chapter 1. – with the exception of 1.5 – and Chapter 2 (see Appendix 4) can be written by the secretary at an early stage, on the basis of the faculty reports. Chapter 3 (the state of the art of the discipline) will require the attention of the committee. In this chapter the committee can put forward its own ideas about the discipline. However, do not wait till the end of all visits, but start thinking about the content at an early stage.

Next to the general report, the public report contains the most important conclusions and recommendations for the faculty. Before the committee makes the report public, a draft version (of those parts which are the concern of the faculty) as well as the general section should be sent to the Faculty Board with the request to amend any factual errors. If no difference of opinion occurs with respect to any factual inaccuracies which may arise, then the committee should adapt the report to take these points into account. However, the borderline between 'factual inaccuracies' and 'coming to an opinion other than that of the committee' cannot always be defined sharply. Should a faculty wish, a reaction from the faculty may be included in the report as an appendix.

4.7 Concluding Remarks

The guidelines given in this chapter are intended to help the review committee, not to make external quality assessment a bureaucratic process. Each committee of experts will tend to look for its own approach; every discipline is different. The guidelines should not be a straitjacket: however, it should take very weighty arguments to deviate from the model proposed. The approach given here will save committee members time and offer faculties a fair assessment.

The committee should not spend too much time describing its ideas about desired developments in their field. Of course, the experts will make use of the opportunity to reflect on them, but these reflections should not delay a rapid feedback to the faculties, who will wish to take immediate action based on the findings of the committee.

Chapter Five

The European
Dimension in EQA

In many countries in Europe we see the development of a national system for EQA, or at least debate about its introduction. In the first part of this chapter an overview is given of the present situation in Europe, partly based on the report *Quality Management and Quality Assurance in European Higher Education* (van Vught and Westerheijden 1993). This report was written at the request of the Commission of the European Union for the Liaison Committee of Rectors Conferences. The Center for Higher Education Policy Studies (CSHOB) of Twente University in the Netherlands has also carried out an investigation into the state of the art of EQA in the member countries of the European Union and the members of the European Trade Association.

In addition, in this chapter we analyze publications of several different assessment agencies. However, the reader should be aware that in such a rapidly changing field like EQA in higher education the situation presented here may not be fully up to date.

Higher education has always had an international orientation; however in the setting of an expanding Europe and an open European market, the need for a European dimension in quality assurance is growing. There is some discussion about the possibility and desirability of European accreditation. The EU has installed an expert group for the development of proposals for a European dimension in external quality assessment (see Section 5.1).

There have been several international programme reviews in the last five years or published in a stage of preparation. In Section 5.2 the importance of such exercises is underlined.

In the last part of this chapter (Section 5.3) an outline will be given for a European system of quality assurance.

5.1 External Quality Assessment in Europe

There are currently several EQA systems in Europe. We may group the countries according to their experience with EQA.

The first group of countries has had substantial experience over at least five years, although not always in the same setting:

- the UK (Kogan 1991, Williams 1992, Frazer 1993)
- France (Staropoli 1992, Ottenwaelter 1993)
- the Netherlands (Hartingsveld 1993a, b; Vroeijenstijn 1993a).

A second group of countries is those with experiences on a smaller scale:

- Belgium, the Flemish community
- Denmark (Evalueringscenteret 1992, Thune 1993a, b)
- Sweden (Nilsson and Näslund 1992, Bauer 1993a, b)
- Finland (Välimaa 1993).

The third group is formed by the countries involved in the discussion, design or try-out of a system for EQA:

- Portugal
- Spain (García, Mora, Rodriguez and Perez 1994)
- several German *Länder* (Frackmann 1993, Webler, Domeyer and Schiebel 1993, Richter 1994)
- Austria
- Switzerland.

The fourth group is the countries which have only started discussion:

- Italy
- Greece
- Belgium (French community)
- Central and East European Countries.

In their study, van Vught and Westerheijden (1993) conclude that the systems in use in Europe have some features in common:

1. There is a managing agency, working at a meta-level. The agent is the coordinator of the system. The meta-level organisation usually has legal status. According to the

Table 5.1. A Comparative Overview of EQA Systems in Practice

	Agency	Why?	Who?	What?	How?	Funding	Use of PIs
UK	Higher Education Quality Council (HEQC), owned by universities	Meta-evaluation Internal quality Management systems	Institutional audits	Especially internal quality assurance processes and policy	Self assessment Peer review Site visits	No direct connection	Yes
	funding councils	accountability quality control quality improvement	subject/discipline assessment	Teaching/learning Research separately	Self assessment Peer review Site visits	Connection with funding	Yes
Ireland	There are plans to introduce formal EQA for the universities. The non-university sector has the National Council for Academic Awards. Institutional audits and accreditation of programmes.						
France	Comité National d'Evaluation (CNE), Independent; directly responsible to the President	Quality control Accountability Assessment of contracts with government	Institutional assessments	Teaching/learning Research Community services combined	a. Institutional: questionnaire site visit	No direct connection with funding, but influence on contracts with government	Yes
			Sometimes subject/discipline assessments		b. Subject: self-assessment peer review site visit	No direct connection	?

Table 5.1. A Comparative Overview of EQA Systems in Practice (continued)

NL	VSNU (association of universities) HBO-raad (association of polytechnics)	quality improvement accountability self-regulation	Subject/discipline assessments	Teaching/learning Research separately	self-assessment peer review site visit	No direct connection	No
Belgium Flemish community French community	VLIR No agency Some discussion about EQA	quality improvement accountability self-regulation	Subject/discipline assessments	Teaching/learning	self-assessment peer review site visit	No	No
Denmark	Evaluerings centeret Governmental	quality improvement accountability self-regulation	Subject/discipline assessments	Teaching/learning	self-assessment peer review site visit	Proposals to connect it with funding	No
Sweden	Office of the University Chancellor	quality improvement accountability self-regulation	Subject/discipline assessments	Teaching/learning	self-assessment peer review site visit	Proposals to connect it with funding	No
Finland	No agency	quality improvement accountability self-regulation	Subject/discipline assessments	Teaching/learning	self-assessment peer review site visit	No direct connections	No
Norway	A system of EQA is under discussion. The Institute for Studies in Research and Higher Education (NAFV) is in charge of the development.						

Table 5.1. A Comparative Overview of EQA Systems in Practice (continued)

Germany	There is no agency. EQA is under discussion and in some *Länder* there are efforts to realize EQA.						
Austria	Starting debate, no formal activities.						
Switzerland	Starting debate, no formal activities.						
Central & Eastern Europe	Many initiatives to come to a system of EQA. In the framework of TEMPUS+ seeking assistance of Western European countries.						
Portugal	Foundation of Portuguese universities	quality improvement accountability self-regulation	Subject/discipline assessments	Teaching/learning	self-assessment peer review site visit	No direct connections	No
Spain	Council of Universities, buffer body formed by all rectors and representatives of national and regional administrations	quality improvement accountability self-regulation	Institutional audit and academic programmes	Teaching/learning Research Management	self-assessment peer review site visit	No	No
Greece	There is no national system for EQA. Discussions are in the direction of the French approach. A sort of CNE is planned.						
Italy	There is a discussion on adopting the French system: a CNE-like committee. Emphasis on the use of performance indicators. No concrete action.						

researchers it is desirable that the organisation acts independently from the government. This is important for the acceptance of the system.

2. All systems are based on self-evaluation or self-assessment. 'Self evaluation is a crucial mechanism for academics to accept a quality management system' (van Vught and Westerheijden 1993).

   Van Vught and Westerheijden do not mention that the way in which the self-evaluation is done varies from country to country. In some cases it cannot be considered as real self-assessment, but should be seen as 'delivering information for the assessment'.

3. All 'models' are based on peer review in one way or another. Experts from outside visit the university/faculty, discussing the self-assessment over a one- or two-day period.

4. A fourth element concerns the reporting of the results. 'Reporting the results of the quality assessment processes is an important mechanism in the process of providing accountability to external constituencies. However, there appear to be various ways of offering such a report and each has its advantages and disadvantages' (Van Vught and Westerheijden 1993).

It is important to look for similarities between models, at the same time being aware of the differences. In Table 5.1 an overview is given regarding the developments in the different countries. Looking at the functioning systems, we see that the differences lie not so much in the 'how' as in the 'why'. All 'models' in practice are based on self-assessment and peer review. Also the guidelines in use for the self-assessment do not differ much.

The first distinction between the systems can be made by looking at the agencies responsible for the external assessment. All of them act independently, but the origin of the agencies are different. In the UK the Scottish, English and Welsh funding councils are government-based, just like the centre for Evaluation in Denmark. In France the CNE is independent, but reports directly to the president. In Finland there is not yet a formal agency responsible for the assessment; however, some experiments are supported by the government. In Sweden the role of the Office of the University

Chancellors is an unusual one. Although government-based, it does not carry out external assessments. The responsibility lies in the institutions themselves. A multi-model approach leaning strongly on local initiatives is used (Bauer 1993a, b). In the Netherlands the agency for the universities (VSNU) and the agency for Higher Vocational Education (HBO-raad) are agencies set up by the institutions themselves; there is no interference from the government. In the Flemish community in Belgium the situation of the agency (the VLIR) is comparable to those in the Netherlands. In Portugal too the Conselho dos Reitores has founded a university-based agency.

We see that all countries have, in one way or another, stressed quality improvement as one of the aims of EQA and accountability as another. The difference is in where the emphasis is laid: more on the improvement side or more on the accountability side. This emphasis also determines the role of performance indicators. It is not surprising that the UK, especially, is occupied with performance indicators because there one is looking in the first instance for accountability. Also, because of the connection with funding, data which is as objective as possible is required.

Another striking aspect of the European scene is that most countries direct the EQA at academic programme level. Only the CNE in France and the HEQC in the UK assess the institute as a whole. In the Netherlands the institutional audit is seen as the responsibility of the individual universities. The VSNU does not have a role in this respect.

Considering the question, 'What will be assessed?', we see that the assessment in general is aiming at the teaching/learning process; when research is assessed in a formalized way, this is done separately. The CNE in France, however, stress that assessment should be done in combination, just as the Spanish universities will do in their try-out.

Most countries publish the reports of the committee. They differ however in size and type of information. The reports of the UK and France are less specific than the Swedish, Danish, Dutch and Flemish reports.

Looking at the overview in Table 5.1 we may conclude that in most countries in Europe quality assessment is high on the agenda. Where there is not yet a functioning system for external quality assessment, people are thinking about it.

5.2 International Programme Reviews

In the last decade, several attempts at an international comparison of programmes have been made:

1. The National Swedish Board for Universities and Colleges in Sweden has carried out an international programme review for Business Administration and Economics study programmes (NBUC 1992).

2. In 1990/1991 an international group of researchers from the CNAA (Council for National Academic Awards, London), HIS (Hochschul-Informations-System, Hanover) and CHEPS (Centre for Higher Education Policy Studies, University of Twente) carried out an international comparison in the field of Economics (Brennan *et al.* 1992).

3. In 1991 the VSNU (Association of Universities in the Netherlands) took the initiative for an international programme review of Electrical Engineering (Vroeijenstijn *et al.* 1992).

4. In 1993 ABET and CHEPS published an international comparison in the field of some Engineering programmes (Goedegebuure *et al.* 1993).

5. In 1993 the initiative was taken for an international programme review of Chemistry, coordinated by the VSNU.

6. There was also an international review of Physical Education in 1993, organised by the Eidgenössische Technische Hochschule in Zürich.

Why international comparison?

There is a lot of interest in what is happening in other countries, but why? One of the reasons is the changing nature of Europe, the growth of a Europe without frontiers. Greater mobility is expected both from graduates searching for employment and from students studying abroad. Higher education institutions will be confronted with the changes. Already many students are studying abroad in the framework of the ERASMUS exchange programmes. Several reasons for international comparison may therefore be identified:

- Competition between universities; it is necessary for a university to assess its quality and the value of the degrees.

- Student exchanges and student mobility require more information about the programmes of other universities.

- Employers will ask questions about the equivalence of degrees: is for example the Master of Electrical Engineering from the ETH in Zürich equivalent to the Master of Electrical Engineering of Imperial College?

Comparing quality we have to:

> emphasise that quality in higher education is multi-dimensional. Thus, attempts to compare the qualities of different programmes, institutions and systems of higher education need not, and should not, involve rankings or the construction of league tables. Particularly when comparisons are international, differences in the context, in purpose and in tradition render any uni-dimensional attempt at comparison impossible. Comparison can at best only identify dimensions of quality within which differences and similarities may be found. That said, however, the multi-dimensionality of quality does not imply the impossibility, at least in principle, of identifying differences in levels of student achievement between programmes, institutions and systems. Levels of student achievement are one dimension of quality. (Brennan and van Vught 1993)

Because all higher education institutions have strengths and weaknesses, it does not make sense to know the quality of an institution. It is far more important to compare programmes leading to a degree. But in comparing degree programmes, we must distinguish between *level*, *standards* and *quality* (Frazer 1992; see also Chapter 1). Too often these three concepts are confused. Comparing programmes internationally, there are three questions:

1. Do graduates from faculty X merit the title? Are they qualified for the title Bachelor or Master?

2. Is this title equivalent to the title in the same field in another university?

3. What is the quality of the programme?

The value of an academic degree depends on the value of the applied academic standards. These standards are fixed by the level of the examinations. The content and level of examinations are fixed by the programme offered; and finally the programme is defined by the formulated goals and aims.

Before we can compare programmes, we must agree on the criteria by which programmes will be compared. For some programmes it will be easier than for others. For technical sciences it will be easier to formulate minimum requirements than, for example, for humanities or social sciences.

International Programme Review Electrical Engineering: an example

As mentioned earlier, the Association of the Universities in the Netherlands initiated in 1991 an International Programme Review Electrical Engineering (IPR-EE). In this project Electrical Engineering faculties from Sweden, Belgium, Germany, the United Kingdom, Switzerland and the Netherlands participated in an evaluation of each other's programmes (Master of Engineering or the equivalent). The purpose was to come to a mutual understanding and recognition of each other's programmes and certificates. The International Committee, in which the academic world, the employers and the professional organizations were represented, evaluated the programmes of the various faculties by an in-depth study of formal material (curricula, examinations, faculty information, etc.). In addition – and probably even more important – subcommittees visited all the faculties at the various sites. The programmes were evaluated against the background of the formulated minimum requirements. The results are published in the report *International Programme Review Electrical Engineering* (Vroeijenstijn *et al.* 1992)

The method used for IPR-EE had four important components: 1. the formulated minimum requirements; 2. a questionnaire for collecting information; 3. a checklist for the assessment by the committee members; and 4. the site visits. Experience gained during three years of external quality assessment of Dutch university programmes was used for the development of the IPR-EE procedure.

THE MINIMUM REQUIREMENTS

At the first plenary meeting, the Committee agreed upon a set of minimum requirements for electrical and similarly named engineering programmes. The proposed programme and general criteria, developed by the IPR-EE Committee, were largely derived from the criteria used by ABET (the Accreditation Board for Engineering and Technology) in the USA (ABET 1991). The minimum requirements concerned general requirements and programme criteria. The curriculum of Electrical Engineering should provide depth and breadth in electrical and electronics engineering. Depth requires the study of at least one area of electrical and electronics engineering at an advanced level. Breadth requires coverage of several areas of electrical and electronics engineering.

The committee also developed detailed requirements for Mathematics and basic sciences, General Engineering Science, Electrical Engineering Sciences, Electrical Engineering Design and Education in non-technical subjects. The general criteria involved the competency of the academic staff and the institutional faculties. The formulated minimum requirements were published in the *Guide for the Committee* (VSNU 1991b) and functioned as a frame of reference during the visits.

THE QUESTIONNAIRE AND THE WRITTEN INFORMATION

The VSNU developed a questionnaire for the faculties in order to obtain information on the programme and the faculty. The questionnaire was sent to the participating faculties. The questionnaire asked for information about:

- the students: level of attainment on entry to the course, entrance selection, dropout rates and completion rates, student workload
- the staff: numbers, teaching load, publication activities
- the programme: the philosophy behind the programme, the goals and aims, the general structure of the programme, thesis work, assessment, quality assurance
- every course: course name, responsible professor, workload, short description of the course, literature used in the course. Respondents were asked to include two examples of the examinations for each course.

The yield of the questionnaire was 22 volumes of information, in total about 6000 pages. All the volumes were a rich source of knowledge about the Electrical Engineering faculties participating in the project. Together with the completed questionnaires, each faculty supplied up to five Masters' theses. Often supplementary information such as catalogues and annual reports was also provided.

THE CHECKLIST

To make possible a formulation of a weighted judgement on quality, a checklist was developed, based on the minimum requirements. The checklist is a translation of the minimum requirements as formulated by the Committee. Members of the Committee gave their assessments of a particular topic on a scale ranging from 1 to 5, where 1 has the meaning 'not satisfactory', 3 means 'satisfactory' and 5 means 'more than satisfactory'. At the end of every visit, the members of the visiting panel completed the list.

THE VISITS

An international programme review cannot be done on the basis of written information only. Additional information and further illustration of the facts supplied is necessary. It is important to sense the climate in a faculty, for example. For that reason the Committee decided to visit each faculty over two days. The purpose of the on-site visit was twofold:

1. It should assess factors that cannot be adequately described in the questionnaire.

2. The team should examine in further detail the material compiled by the institution and relating to: organization of the institution, educational programmes offered and degrees conferred; basis of requirements for admission of students; teaching staff and teaching loads; etc.

The visiting panels consisted of a member from each participating country, but not from the country to be visited.

SOME FINDINGS OF THE COMMITTEE

The committee formulated 16 overall conclusions and recommendations. A selection is given here:

1. All electrical and similarly-named engineering programmes scrutinized meet the minimum requirements

as formulated by the IPR-EE committee. As far as could be judged, the Committee has the impression that the English M.Eng. programmes of 4 years are below the level of the Master of Engineering programmes in West European (mainland) universities.

2. The Committee concludes that electrical engineers graduating from the faculties visited can be considered to be at comparable technical and academic levels. The Committee observed substantial similarities. The Committee believes that the titles used by the faculties visited (e.g. Ingenieur in the Netherlands; Civilingenjör in Sweden; Diplom-Ingenieur in Germany; Dipl. El. Ing. ETH at the ETH, Zürich, Switzerland; and Burgerlijk Electrotechnisch Ingenieur in Belgium) all can translate, in US terminology, to M.Sc. in Electrical Engineering.

3. Although the level of programmes and the standards of the graduates are adequate to excellent, the Committee recommends that the programmes be broadened. More attention should be paid to basic sciences, general engineering sciences and non-technical subjects. The Committee supports the necessity of specialization during the study period. However, this specialization must not be considered as a preparation for future activities in employment. It may rather be seen as a domain in which students can prove their ability to integrate the different disciplines independently.

4. The Committee believes that an effective study period of 5.5 years would seem to be typical for the Western European (mainland) universities. The effective length of the study is fixed, among other things, by the efforts of the students and the organization of the programme. It became clear to the Committee that the nominal study time is too short in the Netherlands. The Committee therefore considers it necessary to change the nominal 4 years to at least 4.5 years, without expanding the curriculum. Such a move would make it possible for many students to study according to the schedule. For further broadening of the programme half a year more would be needed, unless it were done at the expense of specialization, which is not desirable.

5. The Committee pleads for more attention to teaching and for less emphasis on research. Teaching should have the same importance as research in the career of staff members.

6. The Committee recommends that faculties involve industry in programme development and curriculum innovation.

7. The Committee advises that greater exchanges of students and staff should take place between the faculties/departments concerned.

8. The Committee recommends that electrical engineering faculties/departments meet on a regular basis to discuss their programmes and academic standards, both nationally and internationally.

After finishing the project, several advantages of an international programme review can be given:

- The faculties visited get comments of the committee to improve their quality.

- The participating faculties get a deeper insight in each other's programmes: there is common ground for student exchange and mutual recognition of the programmes and titles.

- Non-participating faculties of Electrical Engineering can use the report for the improvement of their programmes.

- Employers in Europe can gain insight into the education of electrical engineers.

Problems with international comparison

The comparison of programmes is already very difficult at national level since the notions about quality are very subjective. According to van der Wende and Kouwenaar (1993):

the problem is compounded when comparison is international, since cultural differences also affect how 'quality' and 'level' are defined. A second problem is that data on which one might base judgements of quality are not available in the same form in all countries, and opinions differ widely on which indicators should be used for measuring quality. Thirdly, the basic elements that make up the structure of educational systems and programmes differ greatly from one country to the next. Even the terms in which these elements are described are subject to interpretation. A fourth problem is the considerable national variation in educational objectives. Fifth is the inevitable problem of subjectivity. Everyone uses their own educational system as their frame of reference for examining and judging other forms.

Although the authors are right, there is no reason not to go further with international programme reviews, keeping the following in mind:

- An international programme review is very complex. Faculties and the experts in the committee must agree on the criteria to be used. For some degree programmes it will be easier than for others.
- Instead of objectivity, national prejudice can play a role.
- An international programme review can never be a paper exercise. A site visit is essential to get a clear insight into the programmes.
- An international programme review is a costly and time-consuming activity. The International Programme Review Electrical Engineering for example took about one year. The members of the committee have together (excluding the secretary) spent more than 260 days. A typical faculty spent at a rough estimate about 50 days in preparation of the information and on the visit.
- Not all faculties are ready for comparison and publication of the results. Sometimes there will be intense resistance not against such a review but against the publication of the findings. A public report is necessary, however, for the sake of the discussion on the programmes and for the information of the outside world. But make sure beforehand that the participants agree upon publication.

In the framework of European quality assurance, such programme reviews will play an important role.

5.3 Some Ideas about European Quality Assessment

International programme reviews may be seen as a pragmatic approach to the European dimension in EQA. Next to it we see the rise of ideas and proposals regarding European quality assessment. Shortly the ideas of accreditation and the ideas of the expert group of the European Union regarding some pilot projects will be discussed.

Towards a European system of quality assessment

In reviewing experiences with quality assessment in several Western European countries, van Vught (1991, 1993) says that it can be argued that in all these systems a number of similar elements are found that can be combined into the core of a European quality assessment system. He stressed that such a system should have a dual function: intrinsic (quality maintenance/enhancement) and extrinsic (accountability), although that will be difficult to achieve.

An element which van Vught considered as crucial in the development of a European system of quality assessment is the idea that there should not be only one coordinating agency. Quality assessment should not be an activity which becomes the bureaucratic monopoly of some new European higher education agency. He pleads for using the experience in the United States with accreditation to design a European system of quality assessment as a system of *multiple accreditation* which implies that there should be a number of agencies, each of which could grant accreditation in the light of its specific objectives and standards. In such a system a higher education institution has the opportunity to seek accreditation with one or more agencies, choosing those agencies that appear to fit best the institution's mission. In such a system higher education institutions also have the opportunity to create what could be called *quality networks*: networks of institutions with related missions and accredited by the same accrediting agencies. The accrediting agencies could differ in the type of standards they would like to emphasize. Some agencies will probably focus on traditional academic standards. Other agencies will perhaps concentrate on specific categories or professional standards (like the professional accrediting bodies in the USA). Some agencies will be directed towards assessment of courses and programmes in higher education. Other agencies might want to concentrate on the quality assessment of research. Again other agencies might try to combine higher education and research. It is important to realize that the idea of multiple accrediting also offers the opportunity to pay attention to the accountability issue and to the extrinsic dimension of quality assessment explicitly. Accrediting agencies may choose to represent specific constituencies and operate for specific audiences (governments, employers, students). In their standards and procedures these specific audiences will then become visible. By choosing specific accrediting agencies, higher education institutions will be able to show to whom they want to be held accountable for their activities and products. Accountability and quality assessment will thus be integrated in a market-like process in which both the higher education institutions and the accrediting agencies have a certain freedom of choice. The accrediting agencies should of course use the various mechanisms and procedures like self-evaluation, external visits, confidential reports. They should perform their coordinating activities at meta-level. Besides, these agencies, like in the United States, should use the mechanism of peer review to formulate the sets of accrediting standards and to decide whether accreditation will or will not be granted. Van Vught concludes: 'Finally, a European system of quality assessment will only come into existence if some international higher education organisations are willing to invest time and energy in its development' (1991).

This idea of van Vught's sounds reasonable. However, a lot of questions remain. How can one convince the national governments to accept the decisions of an accrediting body outside its authority? How will the institutions act? Will they not search for the highest possible accreditation? Which has more value: accreditation by a professional organisation? An institutional accreditation? Accreditation by a student body? Will accreditation in this way lead to harmonization of programmes instead of diversity? To conservatism instead of flexibility?

A European pilot project

Following advice from the Liaison Committee of Rectors' Conferences, the European Union installed in April 1992 an expert group for the development of proposals for a pilot project in European quality assessment. Four experts, coming from UK, France, Denmark and the Netherlands have worked on the report. The terms of references of the group were:

1. to make detailed proposals for a limited number of pilot projects aimed at cooperation in the field of quality assessment in higher education with a view to reinforcing national quality assessment systems and to providing a way to improve the mutual recognition of diplomas and periods of study

2. to include in the proposals details of the objectives of each pilot project, which should emphasize the added-value of cooperation at the European level, the methods to be used and the outline of a possible management structure

3. to ensure that the projects involve cooperation between all Member States

4. to base the proposals upon practice in existing systems of quality assessments

5. to pay particular attention to peer review and to proposals which would assist institutions to establish self-evaluation procedures, for example the preparation of manuals of good practice.

The experts discussed two different models for the pilot projects:

*   an *international* model, involving self-evaluation by the institutions using a common frame of reference followed by site visits by an international peer review committee which would produce an overall report

*   a *two-tier* model with national peer review followed by evaluation of the national reports by an international committee.

The majority of the expert group felt that, given the complexity of any evaluation exercise, it would be better to propose the simplest model (the two-tier model) with a national rather than an international peer review group which would also ensure maximum impact at the national level. The group recommends the establishment of two projects, one for the university sector and one for the non-university sector, each involving one or two institutions from each Member State. One of the major features of the projects is the training function. It was also proposed that a set of guidelines for the self-evaluation and the peer review should be drawn up, based on the common elements in the existing systems.

After the self-assessment a national peer review group would visit the participating institutes. The results would be published in a report which would be translated and submitted to the international committee. This committee would consist of the chairpersons of each national committee together with the members of the expert group. The task of the committee is to discuss the findings and to evaluate the evaluation procedures.

Looking at the ideas developed, the conclusion is that the proposals do not in some respects correspond to the original recommendations of the Liaison Committee. According to the Liaison Committee, the most important objective of the project should be the promotion of cooperation and the European dimension of EQA. The proposals of the expert group start with the question, 'How may each Member State establish a system of QA?' Such promotion of national EQA systems is very important as a first step in coming to a European dimension in EQA (see below). The question is whether this is a task of the European Union. The main question in the framework of the EU should be, 'What can we do at European level that cannot be done at national level?' The proposals are aiming too much at promoting national systems and pay too little attention for the European dimension.

5.4 Towards a European Dimension in EQA

Why is the European dimension wanted?

In November 1991, the Commission of the European Union published the Memorandum on Higher Education in the European Community, the main principles of which were later included in the Maastricht Treaty. The Memorandum says:

> The widening perspectives of higher education institutions in Europe would add a European dimension to the entire question of quality. Quality judgements would tend to influence institutional choices in the establishment of partnerships and participation in networks within European structures and would also be a factor in the granting of academic recognition and hence in facilitating mobility. These judgements will also come into play among students in exercising their choice of institu-

tions and course in a more open and accessible European market for higher education. Employers too will need to exercise quality judgments in a single European labour market in which mobility is underpinned by mutual recognition of diplomas for professional purposes. It is important in this wider perspective that quality is viewed as a larger issue than comparison within and between Member States and that the potential for exchange of experience and for co-operation at Community level in the determination of the parameters of quality and their assessment be exploited as fully as possible. (CEC 1991)

The main question is how to assure quality at a European level. It will never be possible to set up an integral system of European quality assessment/assurance as is done nationwide. However, the national systems will be the spine of European quality assessment. Exchange of students and the recognition of programmes will mostly be based on trust. And it is easier to trust in the quality of another institution when it participates in a national system for quality assessment. Therefore, the condition for European quality assurance will always be the existence of a national EQA system.

European quality assurance: a multilevel approach

A European system for quality assurance will always be characterized by a multilevel approach. The elements will be (see Figure 5.1):

- a good functioning system for internal quality assurance at faculty level and institutional level
- a good functioning system of external programme review or quality assessment at national level
- an external programme review at European level.

The basis for European quality assurance is the existence of a well functioning system of quality assurance at a national level in the European countries. We can already distinguish different systems or models for EQA or programme review in Europe (see Section 5.1). The national systems do not need to be identical, but every system has to meet certain requirements (e.g. the use of self-assessment, combined with peer review; it has to be periodical, covering all degree programmes, transparent and public).

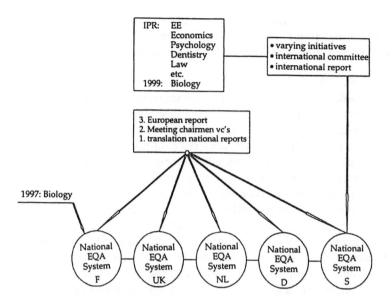

Figure 5.1 European quality assurance: a multilevel approach

To promote the European dimension the following steps have to be taken:

FIRST STEP

Every country develops a good system of EQA. It must be clear that the institutions (faculties) take quality as a serious matter. In designing such a system, one has to take into account the basic principles as given in Chapter 1. For the performance, use can be made of the guidelines in Chapters 3 and 4. When there is an open and transparent system, this will be a basis for trust in each other's programmes.

SECOND STEP

A second step will be for the assessment agencies in the different countries to agree to do the external assessment in the same subject area, discipline or field of study in the same year. At the end the public reports of the committee will be translated into English and

the chairmen of the committees will come together at an international meeting to exchange experiences and to write a European
overview of the assessed fields, based on the national reports.

THIRD STEP

Sometimes an international programme review, as was carried out
for Electrical Engineering, will be desirable. Because a national
assessment does not give a decisive answer about the equivalence
of the certificates from the different countries, it will be desirable
for special disciplines, especially for those fields without European
directives and guidelines, but with an *effectus civilis*, to come to a
European diploma recognition. The method which was used for
Electrical Engineering and will be used for Chemistry is useful for
this purpose. Not all the institutes in a country will need to
participate – possibly two would be sufficient. When the certificates of those two institutes are recognised internationally, it is
possible by coupling the international results with the outcome of
the national reviews to see how far the other faculties comply with
international standards.

Some conditions for European quality assessment

For the development of the European dimension in EQA, some
conditions may be formulated:

- Quality and quality assurance is in the first instance the
  responsibility of the higher education institutions.
- A system for quality assessment and programme review
  should not be imposed upon the higher education
  institutions from above (government, inspectorate or EU)
  but should be the initiative of the universities.
- The role of governments and the European Union is to
  contribute by giving incentives and solving problems
  originating from national laws and regulations.
- Validation and comparison of programmes can only be
  carried out by experts in the field. But employers and
  professional organisations must be invited to participate
  in the peer review.
- The European dimension is essential and international
  programme review is a challenge, but we must be very

cautious that international comparison does not lead to harmonization and uniformity of programmes. That is the paradox of internationalization: student exchanges and validation of parts of the programmes require uniformity in programming. But why should I go to Bologna to study Law when the programme is the same as in Brussels? People should strive after quality and try to keep or to reach the same quality of graduates at the level of Bachelor or Master. However, we must keep the differences and the characteristics of the national cultures.

Appendix One

Short Description of the Dutch University System[1]

The Dutch system for higher education is a binary one. There are:

- 13 universities
- 85 HBO institutions (HBO stands for Higher Vocational Education, comparable to the *Fachhochschule* in Germany; some of them may be called polytechnics)
- 1 Open University, which offers both types of programme on the basis of distance education.

The total number of students in 1993 was 374,000, of which 188,000 were in the HBO sector and 186,000 were in the universities (excluding the Open University). The university with the highest number of students is Utrecht University (25,000 students). The smallest is the Agriculture University of Wageningen (6,000 students).

Since 1993 the universities and HBO institutions have been regulated by the same law, The Higher Education and Research Act (Ministry of Education and Science 1993).

Organizational structure of the university

A university consists of faculties, entities responsible for teaching and research: for example the Faculties of Law, Medicine, Economics, Physics, Mathematics, Social Sciences, Humanities. Every faculty is subdivided into *vakgroepen*, translated as section or research group (see Figure A1.1).

---

1   A great deal of this information is based on the paper 'Structure of the overall educational system in the Netherlands' prepared by Drs D.J.W.M. Mulders for the external assessment of the faculties of Management Studies by the European Foundation for Management Development (EFMD).

Each level – *vakgroep*, faculty and university – has its own executive board. Faculty and university have a council. The council deals with general policy and the budget, the executive board with the implementation of the decisions of the council and with administrative issues. The council, an elected body, is composed of people working or studying within the unit concerned. Society at large is represented on the University Council by members from outside the university.

The Executive Board at the institutional level comprises three members, all appointed by the Minister of Education and Science.

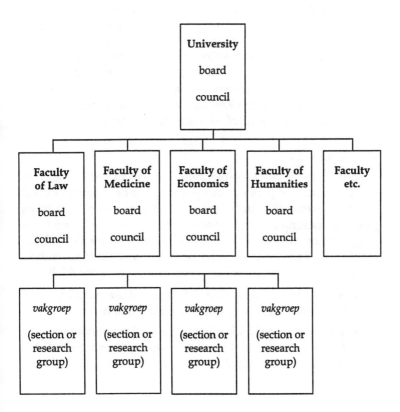

Figure A1.1. Structure of the Dutch University

One is chairman of the Board and one is the University Rector, who also serves as chairman of the Board of Faculty Deans. The third is a member from outside the university. The chairman of the University Council has the right to attend meetings of the Executive Board. Both the University Council and the Executive Board have responsibilities assigned to them by law.

At faculty level there is a Faculty Board and a Faculty Council. The Faculty Board has a maximum of five members, of whom the majority are academic staff. The chairman of the Faculty Board is the Dean, and its members are elected by the Faculty Council. Its responsibilities are the organization and coordination of teaching and research, the preparation and implementation of decisions of the Faculty Council, supervision, the setting up of advisory committees on appointments of chairholders, and to contribute to the Annual Report. The Faculty Council has a maximum of 15 members, at least half from the academic staff. In addition to the Board and the Council, there are two permanent committees: a Standing Committee for Advice on Research and the Opleidingscommissie (curriculum committee) for advice on the curriculum.

The programmes

According to the law all programmes are calculated as 168 credit points, formally equalling four years of full-time study (1 credit point represents 40 hours of study, which includes contact hours, practical training and independent work). Exceptions are initial programmes in certain professional (primarily medical) fields, requiring 210 or 252 credits (five or six years of full-time study).

A programme or curriculum consists of (see Figure A1.2):

- a first, introductory, year, called *propedeuse,* usually concluded with an intermediate examination
- a three-year period leading to the final examinations. Students who complete all the requirements are granted a degree that is defined and protected by law.

1st year	*Propedeuse*:
	selection
	orientation
	propedeuse examination at the end
2nd year	Basic program
3rd year	Specialization
	Optionals
4th year	Specialization
	Master's thesis (final essay)
	doctoraal = Masters examination (Drs; Ir; Mr)
Postgraduate	Teacher education: 1 year
	Designer: 2 years
	PhD: 4 years
	Promotion: 'doctoraat' = Dr.

Figure A1.2. Structure of the Dutch Degree Programme

A regular university programme, comprising 168 credits, is concluded with a *doctoraal* degree. This can be the degree *Drs* (*doctorandus* = he or she who could become doctor), *Ir* (*Ingenieur* (Engineer); the title of the technical universities and the university of agriculture) or *Mr* (*Meester* (Master), a title connected with the Law programme). All three titles *Drs*, *Ir* and *Mr* may be translated by the internationally known title of Master.

In the Dutch situation a formal Bachelor degree does not exist. Dutch university programmes can be defined as so-called 'combined undergraduate/graduate programmes' or as 'long programmes' (as opposed to 'short programmes' such as the MBA programmes common in the United States). Within the Dutch structure, the first two and a half up to three years may be regarded as the undergraduate part of the programme, and the final one up to one and a half years of study as the graduate part of the programme.

The graduate is qualified for a career in research, business or public service. Anyone who has passed the *doctoraal* is eligible to proceed for a doctorate, the title being doctor or dr. (PhD). Apart from the doctorate, there are postgraduate programmes offering specialized training in specific professions, such as teaching and accounting.

The universities provide education in preparation for the independent pursuit of scholarship or the professional application of academic knowledge. University degree programmes therefore combine teaching and research and are, as such, the traditional preparation for admission to the doctorate. *Doctoraal* graduates are expected to be ready to embark on research programmes leading to the doctorate and, in consequence, every *doctoraal* programme must contain an element of research. Research is thoroughly integrated with educational activities, so that most academic staff members are engaged in both teaching and research.

Another feature of *doctoraal* programmes is that they do not contain an introductory phase of general education. Historically, general education has been seen to be the responsibility of secondary education and, as a result, university programmes in the Netherlands concentrate on one field of study from the first year.

The *propedeuse* examination, concluding the first year of the programme, is a selection mechanism, sorting out students who have a reasonable chance of succeeding in that particular programme from those who do not. In each year that follows, there is a growing degree of specialization and – in most programmes – a growing degree of freedom in the choice of subjects.

Instruction is given in the form of lectures, seminars and practical work. Students must pass a specified number of oral and written examinations (*tentamens*) for both the *propedeuse* and *doctoraal* examinations. When they have done so, and have met all other requirements, they have passed the *doctoraal examen* (final examination). In many programmes a *doctoraal* thesis or *scriptie* is required (to translate as final essay, major essay). Sometimes there is a final design or research project, also depending on the field of study. But mostly there is an assignment in which the student can show that they are able to manipulate the acquired knowledge and skills.

Format for the Faculty Report

1. This document is a working document for the committee.
2. It will be sent to the faculty for comments three weeks after the visit at the latest.
3. Most of the information will be processed in the general report. The most important conclusions and recommendations for the faculty will be given.

The Educational Programme _____ in Faculty X of University Z

Date of visit_____

1 Aims and Objectives

1.1 *Aims*

In the text, the committee will comment on the aims. Are they clearly formulated and well known to staff and students? Although the aims and objectives as formulated by the faculty have to be taken as the starting point for the assessment, the committee may discuss them, particularly looking at the academic level and completeness. As far as the committee has formulated minimum requirements, the committee will consider whether the aims cover those requirements.

1.2 *Translation of the aims and objectives in the programme*

What are the characteristics of the programme? Are the objectives recognizable in the programme? Questions to be treated are:

- Is the programme problem-oriented?
- What is the relation between the programme and professional duties in a future job?
- Does the programme further independent learning?
- Is the programme coherent?
- Is the programme up-to-date

2 The Programme

2.1 *The structure of the programme*

In a schematic way the committee will report on the compulsory courses and the credit points. How are the optionals? What are the credit points for the final essay, research assignment, etc.

2.2 *The content of the programme*

The committee will give its opinion about the level and content of the curriculum. What is the structure of the curriculum?

2.3 *Teaching methods*

What is the opinion of the committee about the teaching methods? The ratio between lectures, tutorials, practicals and self-study? Are the most appropriate teaching methods used to realize the objectives?

2.4 *Examinations*

Preliminary examinations and the final exams should reflect the content of the programme. What is the level of the examinations? Are the exams aiming at reproduction of facts and figures or are they aiming at testing insight? Do the examinations test what they are expected to test? What is the frequency of the exams? Are they well spread?

2.5 *Student skills*

A programme should aim at the development of general skills. Is there enough attention to the promotion of written and oral communication skills? Is there enough attention to the teaching of computer skills?

In Chapter 2 the committee will also give its opinion about the preliminary education of the freshmen and the selection/admission policy.

3 Students' Major Essay, Final Research Assignment and/or Practical Training

The major essay and the final assignment are important parts of a study programme. The student should show that he or she is able to integrate and manipulate the knowledge. He or she should show that they are able to act independently. The requirements for the final essay and final assignments reflect the level of the curriculum. Aspects to be treated are:

- the level of the essay/assignment
- the supervision
- regulations regarding practical work.

4 The Student and His or Her Education

4.1 Freshmen and total number of students

In the table the number of freshmen and the total number of students has to be given. Also the percentage of female students. Two years are chosen the year of the assessment and five years before. Are there specific trends (increase or decrease of numbers; participation of female students)?

Table A2.1. Number of Freshmen and Total Number of Students in 1989 and 1994. (All figures used in the table are fictitious)

Freshmen				Total Number of Students			
Total		% Female		Total		% Female	
1989	1994	1989	1994	1989	1994	1989	1994
244	194	2.0%	2.6%	1111	1048	1.1%	2.0%

4.2 *The completion rates*

To gain insight into the completion rates, the committee will give the figure for one student generation (generation of year of assessment minus 8). Are there special trends? (see Table 3.8 on p.80)

4.3 *Average duration of study*

Table A2.2. Average Duration of Study

Year	Average Duration of Study
1991/1992	
1992/1993	
1993/1994	

5 Study Burden

5.1 *Study Burden*

To gain insight into the study burden, how many hours does a student spends on his or her study in reality. How many hours for lectures, tutorials, practicals? How much time is scheduled for thesis and final assignments and how much time does it really take? What is the ratio between contact hours and one's own study time?

It will be difficult to get a clear insight into the real hours spent on the study. Based on the interviews with students and staff, the committee will get an indication.

Table A2.3. Study Burden Calculated in Hours

Lectures/ tutorials	Prac- ticals	Total contact hours	Practical work/ industrial training	Essay final assign- ments	Estimate of real time spent on the study yearly	Estimate of real time spent on the study in total
1449	971	2420	400	1040	1400–1600	7700–8800

5.2 *Information about the study and student counselling*

The following aspects should be treated:

- Information for school leavers
- Information and advice during the study
- Student counselling.

5.3 *Factors hindering the study progress*

In most programmes there are some bottlenecks. What are the bottlenecks for the students in this curriculum? What does the faculty do to prevent them?

6 Facilities

What is the opinion of the committee on:

1. lecture halls
2. working group rooms
3. laboratory equipment
4. practical rooms
5. library
6. computer facilities?

7 The Graduates

In this chapter the committee will give its opinion about the graduates. Do they meet the requirements set for a graduate in this field? Is the curriculum tuned to the labour market? What are the prospects of jobs for the graduates?

8 The Staff

8.1 *Staffing*

Is it possible to teach all the wanted specializations with the present staff? Are there problems with the age profile of the staff? Are there enough members with a PhD? What are the scientific qualifications of the staff?

Table A2.4. Academic and Non-Academic Staff
(Number of Persons and Full-Time Equivalents 1994)

Category	Male	Female	Total		Percentage with PhD
			persons	FTE	
Full professor					
Associate professor					
Assistant professor					
Research assistants					
Others					
Total					

8.2 Student–staff ratio

What is the teaching load of the staff in the calendar year preceding the year of assessment?

Table A2.5. Student–Staff Ratio and Graduate–Staff Ratio

Fte-teaching academic staff	Number of students	Number of graduates	Number of students per staff member, based on fte-teaching (column 1)	number of graduates per staff member, based on fte-teaching (column 1)

8.3 Personnel management

In this chapter the committee will treat the following aspects:

- full professors in the basic curriculum
- didactic qualifications of the staff

- range of specialisation in the staff
- individual assessment of staff members, how is it done?
- didactical requirements to a staff member
- balance between teaching and research.

9 Internationalization

What can be said about:

- international contacts?
- participation in ERASMUS etc?

10 Internal Quality Assurance

10.1 *The self-assessment*

What is the assessment of the committee of the self-assessment by the faculty? Is the report critical and analytical? Does it provide a good insight into the problems? Was the self-assessment report useful for the committee?

10.2. *The preceding assessment*

If the faculty is being visited for a second time, an important question will be: What did the faculty do with the recommendations of the preceding committee? Are the most important shortcomings resolved?

10.3 *Internal quality assurance*

This part is very important. The committee has to give its opinion on the way the faculty takes care of quality. Is there a systematic process of monitoring? Is there a systematic process of evaluation? Are students involved? Who is responsible for innovations? How are those implemented? Is there a curriculum committee? How does it work?

11 General Conclusions and Recommendations

In this chapter the committee will summarize the conclusions and recommendations.

Checklist for the Committee

Checklist for the Assessment of_____

*Name of the member*_____

*Related to the curriculum*_____

*at the University of*_____

This checklist must be completed by every member of the committee at the end of the visit and handed over to the secretary.

1 Aims and Objectives

1.1 The aims

1. Are the aims and objectives clearly stated?

unsatisfactory				satisfactory			excellent		
1	2	3	4	5	6	7	8	9	10

2. Are the aims and objectives a good mixture of scientific orientation and practice orientation?

unsatisfactory				satisfactory			excellent		
1	2	3	4	5	6	7	8	9	10

3. Are the formulated aims and objectives for an academic programme clearly distinct from those of vocational training?

unsatisfactory				satisfactory			excellent		
1	2	3	4	5	6	7	8	9	10

Remarks

_____
_____
_____
_____

4. Are the formulated aims and objectives realistic and achievable, looking at the boundary conditions like the nominal duration of study and the starting level of the students?

unsatisfactory				satisfactory			excellent		
1	2	3	4	5	6	7	8	9	10

5. Do the aims and objectives represent the minimal requirements as formulated by the committee?

unsatisfactory				satisfactory			excellent		
1	2	3	4	5	6	7	8	9	10

6. Are staff and students acquainted with the aims and objectives?

unsatisfactory				satisfactory			excellent		
1	2	3	4	5	6	7	8	9	10

Remarks

_____

_____

_____

_____

1.2 Translation of the aims and objectives in the programme

1. Does the programme offer enough possibilities to develop a capability for problem-solving?

unsatisfactory				satisfactory			excellent		
1	2	3	4	5	6	7	8	9	10

2. Does the programme offer enough possibilities to develop an understanding of the relation between the programme and professional duties in the future job?

unsatisfactory				satisfactory			excellent		
1	2	3	4	5	6	7	8	9	10

3. Does the programme offer enough possibilities to develop an ability to maintain professional competency through lifelong learning?

unsatisfactory				satisfactory			excellent		
1	2	3	4	5	6	7	8	9	10

4. Does the programme further independent and critical thinking?

unsatisfactory				satisfactory			excellent		
1	2	3	4	5	6	7	8	9	10

5. Does the programme further independent learning and work?
6. Is the programme coherent?
7. Is the programme up-to-date?

2 The Programme

2.1 *The structure and content of the programme*

1. Are the aims and objectives translated in the programme in an adequate way?
2. Does the programme contain the necessary basic courses?
3. Is the level of the basic courses satisfactory?
4. Is the supply of optional subjects satisfactory?
5. Can the programme in general be assessed as being at academic level?

2.2 *Teaching methods*

1. Is the ratio between the different teaching methods (lectures, tutorials, practicals and self-study) at an optimum?
2. Are the possibilities to use the computer in education utilized satisfactorily?

2.3 *Examinations*

1. Do the preliminary examinations and final examinations reflect the content of the curriculum?
2. Is the level of examinations satisfactory?
3. Are the frequency and the sequence of the preliminary examinations correct?

4. Are the exam procedures correct?

2.4 *Student skills*

1. Is the attention to written communication satisfactory?
2. Is the attention to oral communication satisfactory?
3. Are the experiences of the students in using the computer satisfactory?
4. Are the laboratory experiences of the students satisfactory?

3 Students' Final Essay, Final Research Assignment and/or Practical Training

1. Is the level of the final essay satisfactory?
2. Is the supervision of the essay is adequate?
3. Do the requirements with regard to the final work reflect the weight of this part of the study?
4. When there is practical training, are the regulations satisfactory?

4 The Student and His or Her Education

1. Is the preliminary education of the freshman adequate?
2. Is the selection of students adequate?
3. Is the dropout rate in the first year acceptable?
4. Is the overall pass rate satisfactory?
5. What is the opinion of the committee about the average duration of the study?
6. Does the programmed study load fit in with the real study load?
7. Can the majority of students finish the study in the programmed time?

5 Facilities

1. Are the student teaching and laboratory areas adequate?
2. On the whole is the equipment used essentially for teaching purposes adequate?
3. Are the library resource materials available to staff and students adequate?
4. Are the computer facilities available to staff and students adequate?
5. Do the laboratory facilities reflect the requirements of the programme satisfactorily?
6. Are the facilities available to staff and students accessible after hours?

6 The Graduates

1. Does the graduate deserve the Master's title?
2. Is the graduate satisfactorily equipped for the labour market?
3. Do the graduates very easily get a job?

7 The Staff

1. Are the competency and qualifications of the academic staff satisfactory?
2. Is the level of scholarship as shown by scientific and professional publications satisfactory?
3. Is the size of the academic staff large enough to cover all of the curricular areas?
4. Is the balance between research and teaching responsibilities of academic staff satisfactory?
5. Are staff development programmes satisfactory?
6. Is the student/staff rate satisfactory?
7. Is the number of professors in the basic courses satisfactory?
8. Is the attention to education and research well-balanced?

8 Internationalization

1. Does the faculty participate in ERASMUS and other European exchange schemes?
2. How involved is the faculty with internationalization?

9 Internal Quality Assurance

9.1 *The self-assessment*

1. Was the self-assessment critical and analytical?
2. Was the self-assessment useful for the committee?

9.2 *Internal quality assurance*

1. Does the faculty maintain a formal and systematic record student progress?
2. Does the faculty maintain a formal and systematic record of initial employment of graduates?
3. Does the faculty maintain a formal and systematic record of staff research and development grants?
4. Does the faculty maintain a formal and systematic record of staff publications?
5. Does the faculty have a good evaluation system, including student evaluation?
6. Does there exist a good climate for regular quality assurance?

Format for the Final Report

I The Review of the Educational Programme

I.1 Introduction

I.2 The involved faculties/departments

I.3 The committee

I.3.1 Composition of the committee

I.3.2 Terms of reference

I.3.3 The working method

I.4 The checklist

For the presentation of the outcomes, the marks are translated into the following symbols:

a score of less than 4	$--$ = critical
a score of 4–5	$-$ = unsatisfactory
a score of 6	□ = satisfactory
a score of 7–8	$++$ = good
a score over 8	⊕ = excellent

I.5 Short evaluation of the review

Ii The Frame of Reference

II.1 Introduction (How has the frame of reference been achieved ?)

II.2 Minimum requirements for the curriculum (in academic terms and professional terms)

II.3 Minimum requirements for the content of the programme (compulsory courses)

II.4 Minimum requirements regarding the skills of the graduates

II.5 Minimum requirements regarding facilities and infrastructure

Iii State of the Art Regarding the Discipline

In this chapter the committee will give a general description of the discipline, in a national and when possible in an international perspective. Strong and weak points of the field.

1 Programme: Goals, Characteristics and Content

1.1 *Aims and objectives*

To verify whether one is realizing within the curriculum what one wants to realize, the implicit aims in well-formulated goals must be made explicit. The Committee should try to find an answer to the following questions:

- Are the aims and objectives clearly stated?
- Are the formulated aims and objectives realistic and achievable, in view of boundary conditions such as nominal duration of the study and the starting level of the students?
- Do the formulated aims and objectives contain a good mixture of scientific orientation and practice orientation?
- Do the formulated aims and objectives meet the minimal requirements? (see Table 4.7, p.105)

1.2 *Programme characteristics*

To formulate goals and objectives is one thing, to translate them into programme content is another. The curriculum must reflect the objectives. What are the characteristics of the programme? Are the objectives recognizable in the programme? Questions to be treated are:

- Is the programme problem-oriented?
- What is the relation between the programme and professional duties in a future job?
- Does the programme further independent learning
- Is the programme coherent?
- Is the programme up-to-date

Table A4.1. Characteristics of the Programme

Programme characteristics	A	B	C	D	E	F
Problem-solving oriented	++	++	++	□	++	++
Understanding relationship between society and the profession	□	⊕	–	–	–	–
Educational preparedness for life-long learning	□	□	++	⊕	++	□
Coherency of the programme	□	□	□	□	⊕	□
The programme is up-to-date	□	□	□	□	⊕	□

– – = critical; – = unsatisfactory; □ = satisfactory; + + = good;
⊕ = excellent

2 The Programme

2.1 *The structure and content of the programme*

In this chapter the committee will give its opinion on the weight of every subject in the curriculum. Is there enough time spent on subject X, too little time on Y, too much on Z? The committee will also assess the level of every compulsory subject.

**Table A4.2. Time Spent on Different Subjects
as % of Total Contact Hours**

Faculty	A	B	C	D	E	F
Subject…						
Subject…						
etc.						

2.2 *Teaching methods*

What is the opinion of the committee about the teaching methods? The ratio between lectures, tutorials, practicals and self-study? Are

**TableA4.3. Content of the Programme
(Example is from an Electrical Engineering Programme)**

Programme content	A	B	C	D	E	F
Mathematics	□	++	□	⊕	⊕	⊕
Basic sciences	□	□	□	++	++	□
Supply of optional subjects						
etc.	□	□	++	⊕	□	⊕

– – = critical; – = unsatisfactory; □ = satisfactory; + + = good;
⊕ = excellent

the most appropriate teaching methods used to realize the objectives?

2.3 Examinations

Preliminary examinations and the final exams should reflect the content of the programme. What is the level of the examinations? Are the exams aiming at reproduction of facts and figures or are they aiming at testing insight? Do the examinations test what it is expected that they will test? What is the frequency of the exams? Are they well spread?

Table A4.4. The Examinations

Examinations	A	B	C	D	E	F
Level examinations	++	□	□	□	□	□
Examinations/goals	□	□	□	□	++	++
Procedures for examination	□	□	□	□	++	□

– – = critical; – = unsatisfactory; □ = satisfactory; + + = good;
⊕ = excellent

2.4 Student skills

A programme should aim at the development of general skills. Is there enough attention to the promotion of written and oral communication skills? Is there enough attention to the teaching of computer skills?

Table A4.5. Student Skills

Student skills	A	B	C	D	E	F
Laboratory experience	++	□	□	++	⊕	⊕
Computer experience	⊕	□	□	□	⊕	⊕
Written communication	++	□	□	□	□	□
Oral communication	□	□	□	□	□	□

– – = critical; – = unsatisfactory; □ = satisfactory; + + = good;
⊕ = excellent

3 Students' Final Essay, Final Research Assignment and/or Practical Training

The major essay and the final assignment are important parts of a study programme. The student should show that he or she is able to integrate and manipulate the knowledge. He or she should show that they are able to act independently. The requirements for the final essay and final assignments reflect the level of the curriculum. Aspects to be treated are:

- the level of the essay/assignment
- the supervision
- regulations regarding practical work.

Table A4.6. Hours Programmed for the Final Essay

	A	B	C	D	E	F
Programmed hours for final essay	1040	1000	950	800	600	1040

4 The Student and his or her Education

4.1 *Freshmen and total number of students*

In the table the number of freshmen and the total number of students has to be given. Also the % of female students. Two years are chosen: the year of the assessment and five years before. Are there specific trends (increase or decrease of numbers; participation of female students)?

TableA4.7. Number of Freshmen and Total Number of Students

Faculty	Number Of Freshmen				Total Number Of Students			
	Total		% Female		Total		% Female	
	1985	1990	1985	1990	1985	1990	1985	1990
A	244	194	2.0%	2.6%	1111	1048	1.1%	2.0%
B	146	152	2.1%	4.6%	776	763	1.2%	2.1%
C	348	247	1.7%	3.2%	1497	1433	1.7%	3.4%
D	229	219	7.0%	9.0%	1086	1063	9.0%	10.0%
E	156	186	10.9%	4.3%	750	1150	?	?
F	748	625	?	6.9%	3191	3573	?	4.6%

In this chapter the committee will also give its opinion about the preliminary education of the freshmen and the selection/admission policy.

Table A4.8. Applicants and Intake 1985 and 1990

Faculty	1985		1990	
	Applicants	Intake	Applicants	Intake
A	244	244	194	194
B	146	146	152	152
C	348	348	247	247
D	251	229	741	217
E	351	239	841	317
F	666	156	1360	186

4.2 *The completion rates*

To gain insight into the completion rates, the committee will give the figure for one student generation (generation of year of assessment minus 8). Are there special trends? The figures for dropout after one year have to be surveyed to determine how selective the first year is. Dropout rate may be defined as the percentage of students who are no longer officially registered as students in the programme after one year.

Table A4.9. Dropout Rates and Graduates for the Student Generations 1988/89

	Freshmen	Dropout after 1 year	Completion rate in nominal time	Completion rate after 6 years	Completion rate after more than 6 years	PhD 10 years
A	187	24.0%	1.0%	44.0%	57.0%	5.0%
B	152	28.2%	7.0%	41.0%	45.0%	7.5%
C	191	29.0%	4.0%	43.0%	54.0%	15%
D	230	3.0%	45.0%	60.0%	65.0%	8.0%
E	227	15.0%	60.0%	63.0%	65.0%	9.0%
F	127	14.0%	61.0%	63.0%	65.0%	9.0%

4.3 *Average duration of study*

Table A4.10. Nominal Duration of the Master's Programme and the Effective Length of Study

Faculty	Nominal	Effective	Discrepancy Nominal-effective
A	4.0	5.5	37.5%
B	4.0	5.9	47.5%
C	4.0	5.7	42.5%
D	4.0	5.5	37.5%
E	4.0	5.9	47.5%
F	4.0	5.7	42.5%

5 Study Burden

5.1 *Study burden*

To gain insight into the study burden, how many hours does a student spend on his or her study in reality. How many hours for lectures, tutorials, practicals? How much time is programmed for thesis and final assignments and how much time does it really take? What is the ratio between contact hours and self-study?

It will be difficult to get a clear insight into the real hours spent on the study. Based on the interviews with students and staff, the committee will have some indication of this.

Table A4.11. Study Burden

	Lec-tures	Prac-ticals hours	Total contact training	Indus-trial	Thesis	Total programmed hours (including individual study)	Estimate of real time spent on the study yearly	Estimate of real time spent on the study in total
A	1449	971	2420	400	1040	6720	1400	7700
B	1744	706	2550	400	1000	6500	1400	8260
C	1579	551	2130	400	950	6720	1400	7980
D	2250	508	2758	680	800	7200	1800	8820
E	2089	505	2594	680	600	7200	1600	8120
F	1937	351	2288	1040	1040	8600	1800	10,620

5.2 *Information about the study and student counselling*

The following aspects should be treated:

- Information for school leavers
- Information and advice during the study
- Student counselling.

5.3 *Factors hindering the study progress*

In most programmes there are some bottlenecks. What are the bottlenecks for the students in this curriculum? What does the faculty to prevent them?

6 Facilities

What is the opinion of the committee on:

- lecture halls
- working group rooms
- laboratory equipment
- practical rooms
- library
- computer facilities?

Table A4.12. Facilities

Facilities	A	B	C	D	E	F
Teaching/laboratories	++	□	++	++	⊕	++
Laboratory equipment	++	□	++	++	⊕	□
Research equipment	++	++	++	++	⊕	⊕
Computer facilities	++	□	++	++	++	⊕

–– = critical; – = unsatisfactory; □ = satisfactory; + + = good; ⊕ = excellent

7 The Graduates

In this chapter the committee will give its opinion about the graduates. Do they meet the requirements set for a graduate in this field? Is the curriculum tuned to the labour market? What are the prospects of jobs for the graduates?

8 The Staff

8.1 Staffing

Is it possible to teach all the wanted specializations with the present staff? Are there problems with the age profile of the staff? Are there enough members with a PhD? What are the scientific qualifications of the staff?

Table A4.13. Academic and Non-Academic Staff: Number of Persons (X) and Full-Time Equivalents (Y)

	Number of Persons and Full-time Equivalents						
	Full professors	Associate professors	Assistant professor	Research assistant	Others	total academic staff	Non-academic staff
A X (Y)							
B							
C							
D							
E							
F							

8.2 Student–staff ratio

What is the teaching load of the staff? Table A4.14 relates the size of staff to the number of students. The faculties were requested to calculate the amount of time staff members spend on teaching, including the time required for preparation and examinations. The

Table A4.14. Student/Staff Ratio and Graduate/Staff Ratio 1990

	FTE-teaching academic staff	Number of students	Number of graduates	Number of students per staff member	Number of graduates per staff member
A	36	1048	124	29	3.4
B	27	763	68	28	2.5
C	48	1433	208	30	4.3
D	27	763	68	28	2.5
E	48	1433	208	30	4.3
F	50	1063	160	21	3.2

teaching load of the entire staff can also be calculated by transforming the total amount of time spent on teaching by all the academic staff to full-time teaching equivalents. One full-time equivalent (FTE) is valued at 40 hours. The total number of students is divided by the FTE-teaching.

How effective is the teaching? Although care must be taken not to attach too much significance to the figures, the number of graduates per FTE-teaching staff provides some information on the results of the effort invested in teaching.

8.3 Personnel management

In this chapter the committee will treat the following aspects:
- full professors in the basic curriculum
- didactic qualifications of the staff
- range of specialisation in the staff
- individual assessment of staff members, how is it done?
- didactical requirements to a staff member
- balance between teaching and research.

Table A4.15. The Academic Staff

Academic Staff	A	B	C	D	E	F
Competency/qualification staff	□	□	++	⊕	++	⊕
Scientific/professional publications	□	□	++	++	□	⊕
Range of specialization of the staff	□	□	++	++	++	++
Size of staff	++	□	++	□	–	⊕
Balance research and teaching	□	–	–	□	□	++

– – = critical; – = unsatisfactory; □ = satisfactory; + + = good; ⊕ = excellent

9 Internationalization

What can be said about international contacts, participation in ERASMUS etc.?

10 Internal Quality Assurance

10.1 *The self-assessment*

What is the opinion of the committee about the self-assessment? Is the report critical and analytical? Does it provide a good insight into the problems? Was the self-assessment report useful for the committee?

10.2 *The previous assessment*

Table A4.16. Internal Quality Assurance

Quality Assurance	A	B	C	D	E	F
Procedures for curriculum design/ renovation	□	++	++	□	–	□
Staff development programmes	–	–	□	□	–	–
Systematic report of student progress	□	□	□	□	□	–
Systematic report of initial employment	–	□	–	–	–	–
Systematic report of staff's R&D grants	–	++	□	□	□	–
Systematic report of staff's publications	□	□	□	□	□	□
Adequate evaluation system	□	□	□	□	□	–
Climate for regular quality assurance	□	□	□	□	–	–

– – = critical; – = unsatisfactory; □ = satisfactory; + + = good;
⊕ = excellent

If the faculty is being visited for a second time, an important question will be: What did the faculty do with the recommendations of the preceding committee? Are the most important shortcomings resolved?

10.3 Internal quality assurance

This part is very important. The committee has to give its opinion on the way the faculty takes care of quality. Is there a systematic process of monitoring? Is there a systematic process of evaluation? Are students involved? Who is responsible for innovations? How are those implemented? Is there a curriculum committee? How does it work?

11 General Conclusions and Recommendations

In this chapter the committee will summarize the conclusions and recommendations.

Format for the Curriculum Description

Curriculum Description

Use *one* form for every year of the curriculum

YEAR:_____

Course number	Course (subject) name	Number of hours for:				Credit points
		Lectures	*Tutorials*	*Practical*	*Others*	
xxxx	Total					

Appendix 6

An Approach for a Faculty Assessment

As indicated in Section 1.6 it might be preferable to assess the whole faculty, rather than an individual programme or correlated programmes, particularly in the case of a very segmented faculty with many programmes. Of course, one could be satisfied with just an audit of the faculty, that is to say one will look only at the quality assurance mechanism in the faculty, but it might be more useful to try to combine the audit with an assessment. There are advantages to a detailed consideration of a single programme: on the other hand one might gain more by considering the connection between the different programmes. The working method described below is based on the method described in this book, with some adaptation. The problem will be that not only should the faculty board and faculty management be assessed, but also the separate programmes.

A The Programme

1 What do people responsible for a programme expect from the assessment?

A judgement on:

- the content, level and coherency of the programme
- the feasibility of the programme
- the quality of the graduates
- the connection between teaching and research.

2 *What aspects of self-assessment should the unit organizing the programme consider?*

The checklist as given in Chapter 3 will be considerably reduced. Only the most essential aspects will be treated. For every programme in the faculty the following aspects should be treated, however:

- Why is the programme offered in the way that it is? What is it hoped to achieve with this programme? What is expected from the graduates? Answering those questions goes far beyond the formal formulated goals and objectives, but asks for the philosophy behind the programme.

- How are the expectations translated in the programme? One should clearly point out how one plans to achieve certain objectives. What knowledge, attitudes and skills are being pursued?

- In what way will the programme be assessed to ascertain whether the goals are realized?

- What are the prospects for employment of the graduates, and for what type of job?

- How is the quality of the programme safeguarded? Who is responsible for innovations in the programme? How is it done?

- In the case of a previous assessment: what has been done with the recommendations?

- How does the unit responsible for the programme regard the relation between teaching/learning and research?

3 *How will the judgements on the programme be achieved?*

Normally, a programme assessment will be done by experts in the field, based on the self-assessment and on a site visit, but it will be impossible to have a separate committee with a site visit for every programme. This would mean that the faculty would be troubled by too many committees. Therefore, the review committee which visits the faculty should make use of previously formulated opinions. It may use:

1. **Written judgements by an expert panel for each programme.**
   Three experts in the field of the programme will receive the
   self-assessment, the syllabus and some final essays (if any).
   Based on this information the panel will give its opinion in a
   report:

   a. The programme may be considered as satisfactory.

   b. The programme needs special attention regarding certain
      aspects. The review committee will be asked to pay
      attention to these.

   c. The programme may be considered as precarious. The
      panel recommends a separate assessment for the
      programme.

   Criteria used for the judgements are:

   a. Are goals and aims clearly formulated?

   b. Have the goals and aims been translated in the programme?

   c. Does the programme inspire confidence in the possibility of
      achieving the goals?

   d. Are the opinions of the students reassuring (see the student
      inquiry below)?

   e. If applicable to this programme: how have the
      recommendations of preceding assessments been dealt
      with?

2. **A student inquiry.** The review committee will not have time
   to talk with many students during the site visit. However,
   students are a good resource for finding out about teaching,
   study load, etc. Therefore, supplementary information can be
   collected by a student inquiry among all students. The panels
   of experts will use the outcomes and also the review
   committee will use them to decide on the students they
   would like to see.

3. **An inquiry among recent graduates (from the last two years).**
   An inquiry among graduates of the last two years will
   supply valuable information about the position of the
   graduates on the labour market, the value of the programme
   for getting a job, the tuning of the programme to the
   expectations of the labour market.

4. **A staff inquiry.** Just as the students will be asked to give their opinion about the programme, an inquiry among the staff will also provide information about the programme and the management.

B The Faculty

1 *What does the faculty board expect from the assessment?*

A judgement on:

1. the mission and profile of the faculty
2. the connection between the programmes offered
3. the research profile
4. teaching and research performance
5. management for education and research.

2 *What aspects of self-assessment should the faculty consider?*

The self-assessments of the units responsible for the programme are directed at the content of the programme. The self-assessment of the faculty should direct itself to aspects and topics beyond the programme level. The following topics should be treated:

1. **Mission and profile.**
   a. the mission statement and the profile pursued by the faculty
   b. educational and research policy
   c. the policy regarding internationalization.

2. **Management.**
   a. personnel management
   b. time spent on teaching and on research
   c. qualifications of the staff
   d. staff development activities
   c. the role of various committees
   d. facilities
   e. internal quality assurance mechanism
   f. student counselling and advising.

3. **Output**

    a. enrolment figures

    b. success rates

    c. dropouts

    d. duration of study.

3 How will the judgements on the faculty be achieved?

There will be one review committee for the assessment of the faculty. This committee will make use of the reports of the programme panels, the outcomes of the inquiries and the self-assessment of the faculty. The committee will have about 7 – 9 members plus a secretary. The committee should comprise:

- a chairperson, well acquainted with developments in higher education
- 4 – 6 experts in the field covered by the faculty
- an organizational expert
- an educationalist.

The review committee will visit the faculty for three or four days (depending on the size of the faculty). The committee will direct itself especially towards the relation between the programmes, the mission and profile of the faculty and the management. Regarding the assessment of programmes, the committee will act selectively. The committee use the panel reports as a basis and talk with staff and students of the programmes being assessed as 'precarious'.

During the site visit the committee will have interviews with the writers of the self-assessment, faculty board, the various committees responsible for teaching and/or research, and with a selection of staff members and students.

C The Report

As far as possible the outline for the public report given in Appendix 4 will be followed. Practice will show what information will be included and what not.

Appendix 7

Outline of the EQA System for Research in Dutch Universities[2]

Objectives

The system of quality assessment of university research serves two primary purposes:

1. **quality maintenance and improvement** by the research group itself
2. **management on the basis of quality** by the board of the faculty or university.

The results of the assessment are primarily intended for the research group concerned. Additionally these results afford an important instrument for faculties and universities in the management and support of their research policy. Furthermore the assessment yields results which contribute to:

1. **public accountability** of university research
2. **science policy** of the national government.

From the point of view of the Dutch universities the contribution to public accountability is not a primary goal. In the same way they realize that the assessment results can serve as an important input for science policy of the national government.

Scope and Organisation

The system extends to all directly funded research accounted for in the Scientific Report which each Dutch university has to publish annually. Of course, closely related research projects funded from other sources (e.g. Dutch Research Council, NWO) will also be

---

2   This outline is based on Berendsen (1993)

included in the assessment of the programme. The assessment proceeds per discipline. The Association of Universities has laid down a classification into some 25 disciplines for each of which review committees will be constituted. Also, a schedule for the three years following the trial year has been drawn up. The executive board of each university (or faculty) can decide for itself which programmes are to be submitted to which particular review committee.

The Association provides some coordination in this process in order to avoid recruitment of experts in the same field on different committees.

Assessment of Research Programmes

The system is designed to assess the quality of research programmes. For each programme an assessment is required on each of the following aspects:

1. **Scientific productivity.** Productivity is assessed by reviewing number, scope and impact of scientific publications: PhD theses, scientific publications and, if applicable, professional publications and patents. The production is related to the input of resources and the research capacity available. The position achieved in the forum of peers, both on the national and the global scale, is also regarded as an aspect of productivity. Therefore, note is taken of participation in international projects, membership of editorial boards, invited lectures, visiting professorships, etc.

2. **Scientific relevance** and/or **societal/technological impact.** Assessment of the output produced cannot be considered independently of its relevance: what is the programme's significance for the development of the discipline? Are the issues and approaches chosen adequate and up-to-date with respect to the state of the art in the disciplines and methodologies concerned.

   In disciplines with a strong strategic or applied character this also comprises the impact on society and/or technology: what significance has the research performed for the development of societal and/or technological applications? In the pure sciences the societal and/or technological impact may be of importance, but it need not be taken into account in the assessment.

3. **Viability of the programme.** The assessment must take some account of the development of the programme and the prospects in the near future. As far as possible, the committee should comment on the viability of the issues and approaches chosen. What are the prospects bearing in mind competition both on the national and the global scale? In some areas competitive strength will depend largely on the size ('critical mass') of the research group and the availability of adequate scientific infrastructure.

As shown in the first two aspects emphasis lies on the performance over the past five years. However, the separate aspect 'viability' implies that the review committee also is asked to prognosticate on the performance in the near future. This should strengthen the value and usefulness of the assessment, both for the research group itself and the board of the faculty.

Institutional Assessment

The system is not drawn up for judgements at an institutional level (departments, faculties) or a managerial level (boards of faculties). However, it seems inevitable that such judgements occur, or can be inferred easily, if a set of research programmes out of one institutional unit has been assessed. A faculty can, if it so wishes, ask a review committee explicitly to comment on research policy and research management at the institutional level. This comment is advisory in nature and is conveyed to the executive board in confidence.

Differentiation of Assessment

For every programme the review committee is asked to assess the three aspects (productivity, relevance, viability) each with their own rating on a three-point scale. Commentaries in words will be attached to each rating. The ratings are defined as follows:

1. **insufficient (-)**
   For the aspect concerned the programme fails to meet the quality criteria of good research which accord with international norms.

2. **satisfactory (+)**
   For the aspect concerned the programme meets the quality criteria of good research which accord with international norms.

3. **excellent (++)**
   For the aspect concerned the programme meets the quality criteria of outstanding research which accord with international norms.

The review committee is deliberately not asked to give an overall assessment, summarizing the ratings on the three aspects. It is the intention that sharp distinctions between the three more or less mutually independent aspects should not be blurred.

Process and Report

The process is fully described in a general protocol laid down by the general board of the Association of Universities. In brief the process goes as follows:

1. The Association of Universities announces that an assessment of research quality will take place in a specific discipline. Next all universities are asked to give a listing of the programmes they want to submit. If necessary the Association coordinates these listings, so that a more or less homogeneous set of programmes can be submitted to the review committee.

2. As soon as these listings are available the deans of the faculties involved discuss whether specific additions of modifications of the general protocol are required. The deans also indicate which type of experts should be appointed in the review committee. The Royal Netherlands Academy of Arts and Sciences (KNAW) is subsequently asked to recruit the chair and members of the committee. In general a committee comprises between five and seven members. In principle a majority should come from abroad.

3. The faculties prepare a documentation set for each programme to be submitted. The set consists of key data on input and output, a progress report and an overview of publications. The information is highly standardized (blanks are provided) and limited in size (e.g. the progress report is about four pages long). Note that, in contrast to the quality assessment of education in the Netherlands, no type of self-assessment is required as an input for the external committee.

4. The documentation submitted is split up between the members of the committee. In a preliminary meeting the committee establishes the issues to be addressed in the interviews or during the site visits.

5. Interviews between committee and research leaders are held. In some disciplines a site visit is added to get an impression of the available infrastructure.

6. An interim report with the findings of the committee is compiled. Each faculty receives its own section in order to allow for the amendment of any errors.

7. The committee submits its final report to the faculties involved and to the Association for further publication. Confidential sections, of course, are only submitted to the board of the faculty involved.

Bibliography

Acherman, J. A. (1988) *Quality Assessment by Peer Review*. Utrecht: VSNU.

Ashworth, A. and Harvey, R. (1994) *Assessing Quality in Further and Higher Education*. London: Jessica Kingsley Publishers.

Ax, A. (1990) *The Control and Promotion of Quality*. Paper presented at the 12th Annual European A.I.R. Forum, Lyon, September 9–12.

Ball, C. (1985) What the hell is quality? In C. Ball *Fitness for Purpose*. Guildford: SRHE.

Ball, C. and Halwachi, J. (1987) Performance Indicators in Higher Education. *Higher Education*, 4–16.

Barnett, R. (1992) *Improving Higher Education, Total Quality Care*. London: Open University Press/SRHE.

Bauer, M. (1993a) *Quality Assurance in Swedish Higher Education*. Paper presented at the European Seminar on Quality Assessment, Quality Support Centre of the Open University, London.

Bauer, M. (1993b) *Performance-Based Funding and Institutional Quality Assurance and Development*. Paper presented at the 15th Annual EAIR Forum, Turku, Finland.

Berendsen, G.J.D. (1993) *Quality Assessment of Research in the Netherlands*. Paper presented at the 15th EAIR Forum, Turku, Finland. Utrecht: VSNU.

Bijleveld, R.J. and Goedegebuure, L.C.J. (1989) The paralysing effects of a balanced power. In P.A.M. Massen and F.A. van Vught (eds) *Dutch Higher Education in Transition*. Culemborg: Lemma.

Boetzelaer, J.M. van and Verveld, L. (1990) *Management of Quality in a Dutch University*. Paper presented at the 12th Annual European AIR Forum, Lyon, September 9–12.

Brennan, J., Goedegebuure, L.J.C., Shah, T., Westerheijden, D.F. and Weusthof, P.J. (1992) *Towards a Methodology for Comparative Quality Assessment in European Higher Education*. Enschede: CHEPS.

Brennan, J. and van Vught, F.A.(1993) *Higher Education Quality: A European Dimension.* Higher Education Report 1. London: Quality Support Centre.

Bresters, D.W. and Kalkwijk J.P. Th. (1990) Quality Assessment in Dutch Higher Education: The Role of the Inspectorate. In L.C.J. Goedegebuure, P.A.M. Maassen and D.F. Westerheijden (eds) *Peer Review and Performance Indicators: Quality Assessment in British and Dutch Higher Education.* Utrecht: Lemma.

Cave, M., Hanney, S., Kogan, M. and Trevet, G. (1988) *The Use of Performance Indicators in Higher Education: A Critical Analysis of Developing Practice.* London: Jessica Kingsley Publishers.

CEC (Commission of the European Communities) (1991) *Memorandum on Higher Education in the European Community.* Brussels: CEC

Chairmanship of the National Advisory Boards on Higher Education (1992) *Quality Assessment in Higher Education in Denmark.* Skive: Centraltrykkeriet.

Cook, C.M. (1989) Reflections on the American Experience. In Ministerie van Onderwijs en Wetenschappen: *Verslag van de Conferentie Kwaliteitsbewaking Hoger Onderwijs, Noordwijkerhout, 3 en 4 mei.* Zoetermeer: Ministerie van Onderwijs en Wetenschappen.

Craft, A. (ed) (1992) *Quality Assurance in Higher Education: Proceedings of an International Conference.* London: The Falmer Press.

Dahllöf, U., Harris, J., Shattock, M., Staropoli, A. and in't Veld, R. (1991) *Dimensions of Evaluation in Higher Education.* London: Jessica Kingsley Publishers.

Dochy, F.J.R.C., Segers, M.S.R. and Wijnen, W.H.F.W. (eds) (1990) *Management Information and Performance Indicators in Higher Education: An International Issue.* Assen/Maastricht: Van Gorcum.

Drenth, P.J.D., van Oss, W. and Bernaert, G.F. (1989) Improvement of Education through Internal Evaluation (AMOS). In M. Kogan (ed) *Evaluating Higher Education.* London: Jessica Kingsley Publishers.

Evalueringscenteret, (1992) *Uddannelsesevaluering i Danmark.* Paper at the *Nordisk seminar om uddannelsesevaluering,* Copenhagen.

Ewell, P.T. (1987) *Assessment, Accountability and Improvement: Managing the Contradiction.* National Center for Higher Education Management Systems. (Paper prepared for the American Association for Higher Education.)

Frackmann, E. (1992) The German Experience. In A. Craft (ed) (1992) *Quality Assurance in Higher Education*. London: The Falmer Press.

Frackman, E. and Maassen, P. (eds) (1992) *Towards Excellence in European Higher Education in the 90s*. Proceedings of the 11th European AIR Forum. Utrecht: Lemma.

Frazer, M. (1992) Quality Assurance in Higher Education. In A. Craft (ed) (1992) *Quality Assurance in Higher Education: Proceedings of an International Conference*. London: The Falmer Press.

Frazer, M. (1993) *Assuring Quality in Higher Education: A Blueprint for the Future*. Higher Education Supplement Quality Debate Conference.

Frazer, M. (1994) Quality in Higher Education: An International Perspective. In D. Green (ed) (1994) *What is Quality in Higher Education?* London: SRHE/Open University Press.

Frederiks, M.M.H., Westerheijden D.F. and Weusthof, P.J.M. (1993) *Interne zorg en externe prikkel*. Zoetermeer: Ministerie van Onderwijs en Wetenschappen.

Frissen, P. (1985) De overheid en de kwaliteitsbewaking in het Hoger Onderwijs. In H.J.M. van Berkel, A.E. Bax and J.W. Holleman (eds) (1985) *Kwaliteit van het Hoger Onderwijs: Bewaking en Verbetering*. Amsterdam: Versluys.

García, P., Mora, J.-G., Rodriguez, S. and Perez, J.-J. (1994) *The Institutional Evaluation of the Spanish Universities*. Paper presented at the 15th EAIR Forum, Turku, Finland. Madrid: Consejo de Universidades.

Green, D. (1994) What is Quality in Higher Education? Concepts, Policy and Practice. In D. Green (ed) (1994) *What is Quality in Higher Education?* London: SRHE/Open University Press.

Goedegebuure, L.C.J., Maassen, P.A.M. and Westerheijden, D.F. (eds) (1990) *Peer Review and Performance Indicators: Quality Assessment in British and Dutch Higher Education*. Utrecht: Lemma.

Goedegebuure, L.J.C., Maassen, P.A.M., Philips, T.R. and Polman, M. (1993) *Dutch Engineering Programs in a European Contest: A Comparison of Chemical, Civil and Mechanical Engineering Programs in the Netherlands, Belgium, France, Germany and Switzerland*. Zoetermeer: Ministry of Education and Science.

Hartingsveld, L.M. van (1993a) *External Quality Assessment in Dutch Higher Vocational Education*. Paper for the European seminar on

Quality Assessment, Quality Support Centre, Open University, London.

Hartingsveld, L.M. van (1993b) *The Sectoral Quality Assurance Project HBO in the Netherlands*. 's Gravenhage: Association of Dutch Polytechnics and Colleges.

Harvey, L. and Green, D. (1993) Defining Quality. *Assessment and Evaluation in Higher Education*. Vol.18, 1, 9–34.

Holmer, J., Nelsson, O., Nilsson, K.A., Rovio-Johansson, A. and Aberg, J.-O. (1992) *Sälvvärdering och extren bedömming*. Stockholm: UHÄ.

Inspectie van het Hoger Onderwijs (1989) *Evaluatieplan van de Inspectie Hoger Onderwijs voor de periode 1991–1994*. De Meern: Inspectie van het Hoger Onderwijs.

Inspectie van het Hoger Onderwijs (1990a) *De Inspectie Hoger Onderwijs en haar meta-evaluatie taak binnen het stelsel van kwaliteitszorg in het Hoger Onderwijs*. De Meern: Inspectie van het Hoger Onderwijs.

Inspectie van het Hoger Onderwijs (1990b) *Externe kwaliteitszorg in het WO*, 1989 (External quality assessment in the universities, 1989). De Meern: Inspectie van het Hoger Onderwijs.

Kalkwijk, J.P.Th. (1991) *Quality Assurance in Higher Education in the Netherlands*. Paper presented at the HKCAA International Conference Quality Assurance in Higher Education, Hong Kong, 15–17 July.

Kallenberg, A.J. and Krol-de Grauw (1992) *Visitatie gevisiteerd*. Doctoral thesis. Leiden: University of Leiden.

Kells, H.R. (1988) *Self-Study Processes: A Guide for Postsecondary Institutions*. Third edition. New York: Macmillan.

Kells, H.R. (1989a) *The Future of Self-Regulation in Dutch Higher Education*. Paper presented at the meeting of the Association for University Governance and Management (VUB&M) Utrecht. Twente: CHEPS.

Kells, H.R. (1990) The Inadequacy of Performance Indicators for Higher Education: The Need for a more Comprehensive and Development Construct. In *Higher Education Management* 2, 3 258–270.

Kells, H.R. (1992) *Self-Regulation in Higher Education: A Multi-National Perspective on Collaborative Systems of Quality Assurance and Control*. London: Jessica Kingsley Publishers.

Kells, H.R. (1993) *External Quality Assessment in the Netherlands After Five Years: A Policy Analysis.* Paper delivered 3 March 1993 at the VSNU Congress, Amersfoort, Netherlands.

Kells, H.R. and van Vught, F.A. (1988a) Theoretical and Practical Aspects of a Self-Regulation System for Dutch Higher Education. In *Tijdschrift voor Hoger Onderwijs 6*, 1, February.

Kells. H.R and van Vught, F.A. (eds) (1988b) *Self-Regulation and Program Review in Higher Education: Proceedings of the 9th EAIR Forum.* Culemborg: Lemma.

Keuzegids Hoger Onderwijs (1922–1994) Amsterdam: Waterland van Wezel.

Kogan, M. (ed) (1989) *Evaluating Higher Education.* London: Jessica Kingsley Publishers.

Kogan, M. (1991) *The UK Case Study.* Paper at the CRE 39th Biannual Conference, Utrecht.

Liaison Committee (1993) *Quality Assessment in European Higher Education: A Report on Methods and Mechanisms, and Policy Recommendations to the European Community.* Brussels: EU.

LSVB (1990) *Onderwijs is Meer.* Utrecht: LSVB.

LSVB/ISO (1993) *Kwaliteitszorg, u een zorg?* Utrecht: LSVB.

Lynton, E.A. (1988) The Role of Self-Study in Quality Assessment of Institutions of Higher Education. In Ministerie van Onderwijs en Wetenschappen. *Verslag van de Conferentie Kwaliteitsbewaking Hoger Onderwijs, Noordwijkerhout, 3 en 4 mei.* Zoetermeer: Ministerie van Onderwijs en Wetenschappen.

Maassen, P. (1989) External evaluation in higher education. In Ministerie van Onderwijs en Wetenschappen. *Verslag van de Conferentie Kwaliteitsbewaking Hoger Onderwijs, Noordwijkerhout, 3 en 4 mei.* Zoetermeer: Ministerie van Onderwijs en Wetenschappen.

Maassen, P.A.M. and van Vught, F.A. (1989) Is Government really stepping back? In P.A.M. Maassen and F.A. van Vught (eds) *Dutch Higher education in Transition.* Culemborg: Lemma.

Maassen, P.A.M and Weusthof, P.J.M. (1989) Quality Assessment in Dutch Higher Education. In P.A.M. Maassen and F.A. van Vught (eds) *Dutch Higher Education in Transition.* Lemma: Culemborg.

McClain, C.I., Krueger, D.W. and Taylor, T. (1989) Northeast Missouri State University's Value Added Assessment Program: A Model for Educational Accountability. In M. Kogan (ed) *Evaluating Higher Education.* London: Jessica Kingsley Publishers.

Ministerie van Onderwijs en Wetenschappen (1985) *Hoger Onderwijs: autonomie en kwaliteit.* 's Gravenhage: Staatsuitgeverij.

Ministerie van Onderwijs en Wetenschappen (1989) *Ontwerp Hoger Onderwijs en onderzoek plan 1990.* 's Gravenhage: SDU.

Ministry of Education and Science (1993) *The Netherlands Higher Education and Research Act.* 's Gravenhage: General Affairs Department.

Minzberg, H. (1983) *Structure in Fives: Designing Effective Organizations.* Englewood Cliffs, N.J.: Prentice Hall.

Moodie, G.C. (ed) (1986) *Standards and Criteria in Higher Education.* Guildford: SRHE.

NBUC (1992) *Business Administration and Economics Study Programmes in Swedish Higher Education: An International Perspective.* Stockholm: UHÄ.

Nilsson, K.-A. (1992) *Evaluation for Quality: Notes of Guidance for Higher Education.* Lund, Sweden: Lund University.

Nilsson, K.-A. and Näslund, H. (1992) *Quality Management in Swedish Higher Education: Competition or Cooperation.* Paper presented at the 14th EAIR Forum, Brussels.

Ottenwaelter, M. (1993) *The Approach of the* Comité National D'Evaluation *of France.* Contribution to the European Seminar on Quality Assessment. Quality Support Centre of the Open University, London.

Paardekoper, C.M.M. and Spee, A.A.J. (1990a) A Government Perspective on Quality Assessment in Dutch Higher Education. In L.C.J. Goedegebuure., P.A.M. Maassen and D.F. Westerheijden (eds) *Peer Review and Performance Indicators: Quality Assessment in British and Dutch Higher Education.* Utrecht: CHEPS/Lemma.

Paardekoper, C.M.M. and Spee, A.A.J. (1990b) *Quality Assessment in Higher Education in the Netherlands, A Government Perspective.* Paper presented at the CHEPS conference 'Quality assessment in Higher Education', Utrecht March 16. Utrecht: VSNU.

Pirsig, R.M. (1974) *Zen and the Art of Motorcycle Maintenance.* New York: Morrow.

Richter, R. (1994) Improving Teaching Quality in German Higher Education. In *Higher Education Management 6*, 2.

Roe, E. *et al.* (1986) *Reviewing Academic Performance: Approaches to the Evaluation of Departments and Individuals.* St. Lucia: University of Queensland Press.

Secretariá General del Consejo de Universidades (1993) *Programma experimental de evaluación de la calidad del sistema universitariá.* Madrid: Consejo de Universidades.

Segers, M.S.R., Dochy, F.J.R.C. and Wijnen, W.H.F.W. (1989) *Een set van prestatieindicatoren voor de bestuurlijke omgang tussen overheid en instellingen voor Hoger Onderwijs.* Zoetermeer: Ministerie van Onderwijs en Wetenschappen.

Sizer, J. (1990) Performance Indicators and the management of universities in the UK. In F.J.R.C. Dochy, M.S.R. Segers and W.H.F.W. Wijnen (eds) (1990) *Management Information and Performance Indicators in Higher Education: An International Issue.* Assen/Maastricht: Van Gorcum.

Spaapen, J. (1989) External Assessment of Dutch Research Programmes. In M. Kogan (ed) *Evaluating Higher Education.* London: Jessica Kingsley Publishers.

Spaninks, P. (1990) *Institutional Self-Study in the Contexts of Decision-Making and Communication.* Paper presented at the 12th Annual European A.I.R. Forum, Lyon, September 9–12.

Spee, A.A.J. (1990) *What is New in Quality Assessment in the Netherlands?* Paper presented at the 12th Annual European AIR Forum on Quality and Communication for Improvement, Lyon, September 9–12.

Spee, A.A.J. and Bormans, R. (1991) *Performance Indicators in Government-Institutional Relations.* OECD Thirtieth Special Topic Workshop Performance Indicators in Higher Education, Paris, 24–26 April.

Staropoli, A. (1988) External evaluation in higher education. In Ministerie van Onderwijs en Wetenschappen. *Verslag van de Conferentie Kwaliteitsbewaking Hoger Onderwijs, Noordwijkerhout, 3 en 4 mei.* Zoetermeer: Ministerie van Onderwijs en Wetenschappen.

Staropoli, A. (1992) The French Comité National d'Evaluation. In A. Craft (ed) (1992) *Quality Assurance in Higher Education: Proceedings of an International Conference.* London: The Falmer Press.

Stubbs, W.H. (1994) Quality in Higher Education: a Funding Council Perspective. In D. Green (ed) (1994) *What is Quality in Higher Education?* London: SRHE/Open University Press.

Stuurgroep HOAK (1986) *De opzet van een visitatiestelsel: Een voorstel voor een (proef)protocol.* Utrecht: VSNU.

Thune, C. (1993a) *The Experience with Establishing Procedures for Evaluation and Quality Assurance of Higher Education in Denmark.* Paper presented at the 15th Annual EAIR Forum, Turku, Finland.

Thune, C. (1993b) *Evaluation and Quality Assurance of Higher Education in Denmark: Background, Methods and Experiences.* Copenhagen: Evalueringscenteret.

Välimaa, J. (1993) *Academics on Assessment and Peer Review – Finnish Experience.* Paper presented at the 15th Annual EAIR Forum, Turku, Finland.

Verkenningscommissie Godgeleerdheid (1989) *Rapport van de Verkenningscommissie Godgeleerdheid.* 's Gravenhage: Ministerie van Onderwijs en Wetenschappen.

Visitatiecommissie Pedagogiek en Onderwijskunde (1987) *Voorstellen selectieve krimp en groei bij Pedagogiek en Onderwijskunde.* Gravenhage: Ministerie van Onderwijs en Wetenschappen.

Vroeijenstijn, A.I. (1988) *Reviewing Academic Performance and Quality Assessment in Australian Universities.* Utrecht: VSNU.

Vroeijenstijn, A.I. (1989a) Autonomy and assurance of quality: two sides of one coin. In *Higher Education Research and Development 9*, 1, 1990.

Vroeijenstijn, A.I. (1989b) *External Quality Assessment: A Burden or a Relief for the Faculty?* Paper presented at the Swedish–Dutch seminar, Groningen October 23–27. Utrecht: VSNU.

Vroeijenstijn, A.I. (1990) Self-Regulation Based on Self-Assessment and Peer Review. In *Quality and Communications for Improvement: Proceedings of the 12th European AIR Forum.* Utrecht: Lemma.

Vroeijenstijn, A.I. (1991) *From the North Sea to the Baltic: How to Transfer Dutch Experiences in Quality Assessment into the Finnish Universities.* Paper presented on the conference 'Quality Assessment in Higher Education in Finland', Helsinki 21–22 March.

Vroeijenstijn, A.I. (1992) External Quality Assessment, Servant of two Masters? The Netherlands Perspective. In A. Craft (ed) In *Quality Assurance in Higher Education: Proceedings of an International Conference.* London: The Falmer Press.

Vroeijenstijn, A.I. (1993a) *Current Dutch Policy Towards Assessing Quality in Higher Education.* Keynote at the fifth international conference on assessing quality in Higher Education, Bonn, July 19–21. Utrecht: VSNU.

Vroeijenstijn, A.I. (1993b) *Some Questions (and Answers) About External Quality Assessment.* Paper presented at the International High-Level Consultation on Policy Issues of Quality Assessment and Institutional Accreditation in Higher Education, Oradea, Romania, 5–7 May.

Vroeijenstijn, A.I. (1993c) *Governments and University: Opponents or Allies in Quality Assurance?* Key note at the SRHE-Annual conference.

Vroeijenstijn, A.I. and Acherman, J.A. (1990) Control-Oriented Quality Assessment Versus Improvement-Oriented Quality Assessment. In L.C.J. Goedegebuure, P.A.M. Maassen and D.F. Westerheijden (eds) *Peer Review and Performance Indicators: Quality Assessment in British and Dutch Higher Education.* Utrecht: CHEPS/Lemma.

Vroeijenstijn, A.I., Waumans, B.L.A. and Wijmans, J. (1992) *International Programme Review Electrical Engineering.* Utrecht: VSNU.

VSNU (1989) *Over de kwaliteit van het Nederlands onderwijs.* Utrecht: VSNU.

VSNU (1990a) *Guide to External Program Review.* Utrecht: VSNU.

VSNU (1990b) (Visitatiecommissie Wiskunde en Informatica.) *Rapport waarin de Visitatiecommissie Wiskunde en Informatica haar bevindingen ten aanzien van het onderwijs binnen de studierichtingen Wiskunde en Informatica heeft vastgelegd.* Utrecht: VSNU.

VSNU (1990c) *Kwaliteitszorg binnen het universitair onderwijs: Een tussentijdse rapportage en werkplan 1991–1993.* Utrecht: VSNU.

VSNU (1990d) (Visitatiecommissie Geografie.) *Rapport waarin de Visitatiecommissie Geografie haar bevindingen ten aanzien van het onderwijs binnen de studierichtingen Sociale Geografie, Fysische Geografie, Pre- en Protohistorie, Planologie, en (Niet) Westerse Demografie heeft vastgelegd.* Utrecht: VSNU.

VSNU (1990e) *Bevindingen van de verschillende visitatiecommissies met betrekking tot cursusduur/studieduur en factoren die de studieduur beinvloeden.* Utrecht: VSNU.

VSNU (1990f) (Visitatiecommissie IO en LR.) *Rapport waarin de Visitatiecommissie IO en LR haar bevindingen ten aanzien van het onderwijs binnen de studierichtingen Industrieel Ontwerpen en Luchtvaart- en Ruimtevaarttechniek heeft vastgelegd.* Utrecht: VSNU.

VSNU (1991a) (Visitatiecommissie Elektrotechniek) *Rapport waarin de Visitatiecommissie Elektrotechniek haar bevindingen ten aanzien van het onderwijs binnen de studieniehtingen Elektrotechniek en Informatietechniek heeft vastgelegt.* Utrecht: VSNU.

VSNU (1991b) *IPR-EE: Guide for the Committee.* Utrecht: VSNU.

VSNU (1993a) *Wat was goed en wat kan beter? Meningen en suggesties vanuit visitatiecommissies en disciplineoverlegorganen over de 1e ronde kwaliteitszorg 1988–1993.* Utrecht: VSNU.

VSNU (1993b) *Quality Assessment of Research Protocol 1993.* Utrecht: VSNU.

Vught, F.A. van (1988) A new Autonomy in European Higher Education? In H.R. Kells and F.A. van Vught (eds) *Self-Regulation, Self-Study and Program Review in Higher Education.* Culemborg: Lemma.

Vught, F.A. van (1989) Higher Education in the Netherlands. In P.A.M. Maassen and F.A. van Vught (eds) *Dutch Higher Education in Transition.* Culemborg: Lemma.

Vught, F.A. van (1991) Higher Education Quality Assessment in Europe, next step, *Creaction 1991,* 4, 61–82.

Vught, F.A. van (1993) Towards a general model of quality assessment in higher education. In J. Brennan and F.A. van Vught (1993) *Questions of Quality: In Europe and Beyond.* Higher Education Report No 1. London: Quality Support Centre.

Vught, F.A. van and Westerheijden, D.F. (1993) *Quality Management and Quality Assurance in European Higher Education.* Enschede: CHEPS.

Webb, C. (1994) Quality Audit in the Universities. In D. Green (ed) (1994) *What is Quality in Higher Education?* London: SRHE/Open University Press.

Webler, W.-D., Domeyer, V. and Schiebel, B. (1993) *Lehrberichte, empirische Grundlagen, Indikatorenauswahl und Empfehlungen sur Darstellung der Situation der Lehre in Lehrberichten.* Bonn: Bundesministerium für Bildung und Wissenschaft.

Weiden, M.G.H. van der (1994) *External Quality Assessment and Feasibility of Study Programs.* Utrecht: VSNU.

Wende, M. van der and Kouwenaar, K. (1993) In search of Quality. In *The Quality Debate: A Discussion on the Contribution of International Cooperation to Higher Education.* Limburg: University of Limburg.

Westerheijden, D.F. (1990) *Peers, Performance or Power? A Reflection on the Dutch Quality Assessment System in Higher Education.* Paper presented at the CHEPS conference: 'Quality assessment in Higher Education', Utrecht, March 16. Utrecht: VSNU.

Williams, P. (1992) The UK Academic Audit Unit. In A. Craft (ed) *Quality Assurance in Higher Education: Proceedings of an International Conference*. London: The Falmer Press.

Further Reading

The literature about quality assessment is very extensive. There have been many conferences and seminars where EQA has been discussed. Many of the contributions have circulated informally; some of them find a way into the formally published proceedings. There have also been many books published on the subject, a selection of which is listed here.

Allan Ashworth and Roger Harvey (1994) *Assessing Quality in Further and Higher Education*. London: Jessica Kingsley Publishers. 152 pages and appendices. ISBN 1 85302 539 9.

This book seeks to outline the qualitative aspects of Total Quality Management and to illustrate quantitative measures by which it can be properly evaluated and looks forward to the end of the decade, identifying changes which are expected to occur and which will have an impact upon the post-compulsory educational system. The book is intended for managers of colleges and universities where quality control is exercised, providing a handbook of scientific techniques which will allow managers to maintain and improve their standards of quality. The book covers the following areas: quality and the role of performance indicators; organisation and resources; students; teaching and learning; curriculum; standards and assessment.

Ronald Barnett (1992) *Improving Higher Education: Total Quality Care*. London: SRHE/Open University Press. 217 pages and appendices. ISBN 0 335 09985 8.

This book is, according to the author, 'not a textbook on quality. Nor will those seeking a recipe book for the successful introduction of a quality assurance system in an institution find it in this book'. The book provides a systematic exploration of the topic quality in higher education. It examines the meaning of quality and its improvement at the levels of both the institution and the course – contemporary discussion having tended to focus on one or the other, without integrating the two perspectives. He argues against a simple identification of quality assessment with numerical performance indicators or with academic audit or with the messages of the market. These are the contending definitions of the modern age, but they all contain interests tangential to the main business of higher education.

Dr Barnett offers an alternative approach which begins from a sense of educators attempting to promote an open-ended development in their students. It is this view of higher education which, he argues, should be at the heart of our thinking about quality. Quality cannot be managed, but it can be cared for. Building on the conceptual base he establishes, proposals for action in assessing institutional performance are offered, in reviewing the quality of course programmes, and in improving the curriculum and the character of the student experience.

Alma Craft (1992) *Quality Assurance in Higher Education. Proceedings of an International Conference.* London: The Falmer Press. 250 pages. ISBN 0 75070 070 X.

In 1991, The Hong Kong Council for Academic Accreditation took the initiative to set up an International Network for Quality Assurance Agencies in Higher Education (INQAAHE). The start was given by organizing an international conference. The contributions were published in this book. After an overview by Malcolm Frazer, international developments are given. Throughout, the tension between institutional autonomy and accountability, and between self-assessment and external review, is acknowledged. Most contributors agree that formal external procedures can prevent complacency and can legitimize internal systems in the eyes of the public.

Urban Dahllöf, John Harris, Michael Shattock, André Staropoli and Roeland in't Veld (1991) *Dimensions of Evaluation in Higher Education.* London: Jessica Kingsley Publishers. 192 pages. ISBN 1 85302 526 7.

This book is a report of the IMHE Study Group on Evaluation in Higher Education. It addresses primary issues in evaluation in an international, a national and a long-term perspective. Roeland in't Veld sets the policy frameworks within which the increased emphasis on evaluation must be considered. Michael Shattock analyses the contribution of universities to society. André Staropoli assesses the evaluation of research, something which has become a political priority. Urban Dahllöf reflects on the universally low priority given to the evaluation of teaching and provides a critique of the measures that are being used. John Harris reports on the ways of comparing higher education in the USA with that of competitor nations.

The essays come together to demonstrate that arguments about the nature and techniques of evaluation must entail far broader considerations than those often promoted by policy-makers.

Diana Green (ed) (1994) *What is Quality in Higher Education*? London: SRHE/Open University. 120 pages. ISBN 0 335 15740 8.

For higher education in the UK, the Government is committed to an overt link between quality assessment and funding decisions. However, there is no currently agreed definition of quality; and if there is no consensus about what quality is in higher education, how can it be assessed?

This book was stimulated by, and reflects some of the debate following, the publication of the 1991 Further and Higher Education Bill and its subsequent enactment. It also draws on the preliminary findings of a major national research project funded by a partnership of government, business and higher education, designed to develop and test methods for systematically assessing quality.

The focus in the book is on the quality of teaching and learning. The book illustrates the extent to which quality has overtaken efficiency as the key challenge facing higher education in the 1990s. It underlines the growing awareness that institutions are accountable not only to the government which funds them but also, in an increasingly competitive higher education market, to the customers – the students. The book therefore signals the early stages of what threatens to be cultural revolution as profound as that which has transformed the behaviour of organizations in the manufacturing and commercial sectors.

The contributions of Diana Green 'What is Quality in Higher Education? Concepts, Policy and Practice' and Malcolm Frazer 'Quality in Higher Education: An international perspective' are particularly valuable.

Leo C.J. Goedegebuure, Peter A.M. Maassen and Don F. Westerheijden (eds) (1990) *Peer Review and Performance Indicators: Quality Assessment in British and Dutch Higher Education.* Utrecht: CHEPS. 226 pages. ISBN 90 5 189 054 0.

This book is the result of a conference in 1989, where quality assessment in British and Dutch higher education was compared. Although maybe a little outdated, because of subsequent developments in the UK and the Netherlands, the book still has a value for the discussion on the use of performance indicators and the use of peer review. In several contributions the case for and against is discussed.

H.R. Kells (1992) *Self-Regulation In Higher Education. A Multi-National Perspective on Collaborative Systems of Quality Assurance and Control.* London: Jessica Kingsley Publishers. 163 pages and appendices. ISBN 1 85302 528 3.

This book describes the development and evolution of several major forms of regulatory systems for higher education on both sides of the Atlantic, with particular emphasis on the increasingly complex and self-regulatory intentions and characteristics. It focuses primarily on the nature and the development of evaluation systems as they are experienced in the wider concept of regulation – their attributes, strengths, limits and how they can be improved. It analyses the patterns that are emerging, the apparent national determinants and the critical relationships between purposes and means in the systems. It is intended both as reference source and as a guide for policy-makers in institutions, collaborative organisations and in government seeking to consider the possibilities of self-regulation in higher education. It aims to help achieve the potential benefits of such systems, including the preservation of universities and their autonomy amid the considerable and understandable pressures to make them more effective and efficient. In short, when self-regulation is one of the aims of EQA, this book is a must for the reader to think about the nature of self-regulation, its possibilities and its limits.

H.R. Kells (1988) *Self-Study Processes: A Guide For Post-Secondary Institutions.* (Third edition) New York: Macmillan. ISBN 0 02 917281 0.

This book is a valuable instrument for all who are involved with self-assessment. It covers every aspect of the self-study process, and is filled with informative case studies, tables, charts, diagrams, checklists and tested, step-by-step advice. It is a valuable resource for everyone anxious to realize the potential of self-study as a tool for improving the quality of programmes and institutions.

Maurice Kogan (ed) (1989) *Evaluating Higher Education*. London: Jessica Kingsley Publishers. 220 pages. ISBN 1 85302 5100.

As is always the problem with publications based on conference papers, this book is somewhat outdated. Nevertheless, it contains valuable case studies about the wide range of possible approaches to the evaluation of higher education that can be found at different levers in different systems. The experiences described in this book are drawn from many countries represented in the Organization for Economic Cooperation and Development (OECD).